LOVE ON THE DOLE

Ronald Gow and Walter Greenwood

LOVE ON THE DOLE

Edited by Ray Speakman

THE HEREFORD PLAYS

Heinemann Educational Books

Heinemann Educational Books Ltd
Halley Court, Jordan Hill, Oxford OX2 8EJ
OXFORD   LONDON   EDINBURGH   MELBOURNE
SYDNEY   AUCKLAND   SINGAPORE   MADRID
ATHENS   IBADAN   NAIROBI   GABORONE
HARARE   KINGSTON   PORTSMOUTH (USA)

First published in 1986
Reprinted 1987, 1988

ISBN 0 435 22360 7

Typeset by
Latimer Trend & Company Ltd, Plymouth
Printed in Great Britain by
J. W. Arrowsmith Ltd, Bristol

Contents

Introduction

The time is ripe, and rotten ripe, for change;
Then let it come ...

(James Russell Lowell; quoted by Walter Greenwood as
the epigraph to his novel *Love on the Dole*)

There can have been few plays written in England this
century which have had such an impact upon the general
public as *Love on the Dole*. In more recent times one looks to
plays like *Look Back in Anger*, *Cathy Come Home* or *Boys
from the Blackstuff* in order to come anything like close to
understanding the way in which Ronald Gow's play, from
Walter Greenwood's novel, was received. By the end of
1935 a million people had seen the play on the stage,
reviewers talked of it as having been 'conceived and written
in blood', of being 'sincere and powerful' and 'admirable
and extremely moving'. In the country at large, the Rever-
end Pat McCormick of St Martin's said that after seeing the
play 'he could not sleep and God was calling on him to "do
something" '; Sir Herbert Samuel in the House of Com-
mons urged his fellow Members to go and see this 'very
poignant' play; and two years later, in *The Road to Wigan
Pier*, George Orwell wrote in terms which clearly reflect the
impact which the play made upon him (see below, note 37).
Whether or not Ronald Gow intended his play to have so
polemical a nature in the eyes of his audience is open to
argument: 'One aimed to touch the heart,' he says, and 'I
certainly didn't write a play about unemployment with any
idea of West End production, no one in their senses would
do that.' Nevertheless, the fact is that *Love on the Dole* is a
classic example of a play which, in its time, achieved
triumphantly a social and political relevance which touched
and moved public awareness, and went some way towards
shifting public opinion with regard to unemployment. Indeed, it is a very rare piece of theatre that can be mentioned
in the same breath as an event such as the Jarrow Crusade of
1936. *Love on the Dole* is such a piece and lives in the

memory of many as of equal importance and of equal impact.

Yet to treat the play, and the novel before it, as many critics have, as a 'social document', of interest only as source material for the decade in which it was written, strikes me as perversely unfair and short-sighted. Apart from its clear relevance to the latter part of this century in terms of the play's central issue, I would suggest that the novel has made more than a passing impression upon such writers as Sillitoe, Chaplin and Hines (and others of the 'social realism school' of the late 1950s and the 1960s) and that the play is very much part of a tradition which began, perhaps, with D. H. Lawrence and has continued through to recent writers like Wesker, Plater, Bleasdale, Russell and Godber. Of course, it will be argued that the structure of *Love on the Dole* has more in common with the 'northern' tradition of plays such as *Hobson's Choice* and *Hindle Wakes*, but the subject-matter, the characters portrayed and, particularly, the language – besides being startlingly new at the time of its first performance – are, I would suggest, much closer to the works of those more contemporary writers I have mentioned than to the play's predecessors.

This new edition, then, is made not only because the play is a classic, but also because, as one reviewer said of it at the time of its first performance, 'The matter of the play is here and now,' and because its 'terrible picture of people caught in a trap, hopeless and helpless' is of much more than documentary and historical interest. The 'here and now' of *Love on the Dole* really is here and now – in artistic as well as in social and political terms.

Walter Greenwood was born in the Hankinson Park area of Salford – 'Hanky Park' in the novel – in 1903 and was educated at a local council school as well as 'by self' as he put it. Whilst still at school he worked part-time as a milk-boy and as a pawnbroker's clerk. After school he had various jobs including stable-boy, clerk, packing-case maker, signwriter, cab driver, warehouseman and salesman. Inevitably, he was also out of work and 'on the dole' for part of the time. During these periods of unbidden idleness he wrote short stories, worked for the Salford Labour Party and, eventually, wrote his first novel.

In a later newspaper interview Greenwood said that he was 'burning up inside with fury at the poverty' he saw around him, and in another newspaper he said that in his novel he had 'tried to show what life means to a young man living under the shadow of the dole, the tragedy of a lost generation who are denied consummation, in decency, of the natural hopes and desires of youth'.

After several rejections, the novel was published by Jonathan Cape in June 1933. By July of the same year there was a second impression, by August a third, and by the outbreak of the Second World War in 1939 there had been a further eight impressions in England, publication in the United States and several translations. Contemporary reviews were all enthusiastic; their tone can best be summed up by Edith Sitwell's later comment, in a letter to Walter Greenwood: 'I do not know when I have been so deeply, so terribly moved.' Although he published a further ten novels, a collection of short stories and the autobiographical collection *There Was a Time*, Walter Greenwood's work did not receive such attention again, and he has been sadly neglected by critics. He died in 1974.

Ronald Gow spent much of his childhood in the Rossendale Valley, Lancashire, where he 'knew about the world of clogs and shawls and "trouble up at t'mill". In fact, as the boss's grandson I had the run of one of those mills.' He was reading for a science degree at Manchester University when the First World War began, and before completing his course spent time working in a chemical factory and joined an Officer's Training Unit. After university he taught at Altrincham Grammar School, of which time a former pupil, Douglas Rendell, said: 'No boy is likely to forget his teaching ... he was a very likeable man with the knack of arousing enthusiasm in a lot of people ...' Apart from teaching English and drama, he gained during this period a considerable reputation as a maker of silent films with his pupils.

After writing plays for the BBC in Manchester and for a

local amateur company, Ronald Gow's first London production was *Gallows Glorious* (1933). The play dealt with
the American slave-liberator John Brown, and was
received, according to the *Daily Telegraph* theatre critic, W.
A. Darlington, with 'a tremendous welcome from a wildly
enthusiastic audience ... they cheered and went on cheering'. It was subsequently suggested to him 'that a play of
protest might be written about a contemporary evil, rather
than slavery, and I was asked to read Greenwood's novel,
Love on the Dole'. He immediately felt that 'here was
something that needed writing about, no holds barred'.

Love on the Dole opened at the Manchester Repertory
Theatre in February 1934, after which a group was formed
to send it on tour:

> But there were quite a number of problems on the journey
> from Manchester to London ... After all it was regarded as a
> 'dangerous' play. There were three million unemployed;
> there was trouble about the scandalous Means Test; working
> men were marching on London; and worst of all the play was
> strangely popular. Two separate companies were touring the
> country in the year before the London production. In towns
> where there was no theatre the play was often performed in
> picture houses – twice nightly.
>
> London managements ... would have nothing to do with
> the play. It was not 'West End'. It concerned a social evil
> which they thought a London audience would find depress-
> ing ... Then the Manchester Company ... decided that they
> themselves would take a hand ... all the money they had
> made on tour was ventured on an entirely new production.
> The Garrick Theatre was obtained. Wendy Hiller played
> Sally. Cathleen Nesbitt Mrs Hardcastle ...
>
> (Ronald Gow)

In all, 391 performances were given in London, then the
play went successfully to New York in 1936 and Paris in
1937. Despite the clear success of both the play and the
novel, the British Board of Film Censors would not allow
the story to be filmed in the 1930s: it was 'a very sordid
story in very sordid surroundings', they said. The story was
eventually filmed in 1940, when the climate was obviously

very different, and the clearly stated aim was 'to show the public the true state of affairs which arose after the last war in the industrial areas and which must not be allowed to flourish when the immediate conflict is over' (foreword to the film).

Very little has been written about either the play or the novel. Perhaps the most interesting analysis is given by a historian, Stephen Constantine (see Notes). He argues that, as the play 'blames' no individuals for unemployment, the middle classes, who made up the audience for both play and novel, did not feel threatened by the work but were sufficiently moved to set in motion those social reforms which emerged after the Second World War. Ronald Gow identifies the play's success in these terms: '... one could say that basically it is a good "Peg's Paper" romance. The main villain is unemployment and there is plenty of humour in it and a fundamental British optimism. Another element in the play's success was that for a London audience the characters were working class people – something new.' This typically self-effacing comment from Ronald Gow needs some development. The play was (and still is) relevant – it confronts a contemporary issue sharply and clearly. Constantine's argument that the play reorients the audience without being 'dangerous' is also convincing. What he does not say, nor does Ronald Gow (nor do the rather begrudging critics elsewhere), is that it is a rattling good piece of writing. It is characterised by a scrupulous fidelity to its characters – their ways of seeing and their ways of speaking – and the action of the play arises naturally out of their perceptions and experiences. The particular achievement of the play is that Ronald Gow manages this fidelity whilst at the same time retaining a dramatic drive throughout the piece. It is the play's form which makes a potentially 'dangerous' subject, approached in a 'new' way – with unfamiliar language and alternative perspectives – accessible to an audience. Thus we have the play's success, its impact – its impingement on the lives of so many individuals at the time of its first performances, causing them to see *Love on the Dole*, like the writer of the notice in *News*

Acknowledgement

Special thanks are more than due to Ronald Gow – for his long-suffering assistance in the preparation of this new edition, for his remarkable kindness in sharing so many of his memories and observations, and for his hard work in sorting out and sending me copies of reviews, letters, theatre programme notes, essays and articles.

LOVE ON THE DOLE

CHARACTERS

SALLY HARDCASTLE

LARRY MEATH

MR HARDCASTLE

MRS HARDCASTLE

MRS BULL

MRS DORBELL

MRS JIKE

HELEN HAWKINS

A POLICEMAN

CHARLIE

SAM GRUNDY

A YOUNG MAN

A NEWSBOY

MEN and WOMEN, etc.

Act I

(*The Gods Defied*) The Hardcastles' kitchen in Hanky Park

Act II

Scene 1
(*Interlude*) An alley in Hanky Park
Scene 2
(*Worship in the High Places*) On the moors

Act III

Scene 1
(*Catastrophe*) The Hardcastles' kitchen – a year later
Scene 2
(*Resurrection*) The same – six months later

ACT I

The kitchen living-room of the Hardcastles' at No. 17 North Street, Hanky Park. In the back wall, facing us, is the street door, and beside it a window also overlooks the street. A door on the right (an architectural liberty for stage purposes) leads to the other part of the house. On the left is a small kitchen range. In the corner upstage is a kitchen sink. There is very little furniture, and what there is shows signs of decay and collapse. A plain table in the centre has some rickety chairs beside it. Near the fireplace is a rocking chair, and on the right, downstage, is a dilapidated sofa.

It is important to remember that this is not slum property, but the house of a respectable working man, whose incorrigible snobbery would be aroused if you suggested that North Street was a slum.

SALLY HARDCASTLE, *a fine-looking girl of twenty, is ironing clothes, although the greater part of her interest is centred at the moment on events out in the street. The street door is open, and through the window we can see a speaker addressing a meeting under a neighbouring lamp.*

SALLY *goes to the door and looks out, listening. As her mother enters she hurries back to her ironing.*

MRS HARDCASTLE *enters,[1] from another part of the house, carrying a laundry-basket. She is a nondescript sort of woman who might have been as pretty as* SALLY *in her youth, but a losing fight against drudgery and poverty has played havoc with her womanly grace and character.*

THE SPEAKER: . . . and to find the cost of this present system you have only to look at our own lives and the lives of our parents and their parents. Labour never ending, pawn-shops, misery and dirt. No time for anything bright and beautiful. Grey, depressing streets. Mile after mile of them . . .

A VOICE: Y'can't do without capikle!

(*Groans and laughter*)

THE SPEAKER: Unemployment and pauperdom, that is the legacy of the Industrial Revolution. That is the price we pay for the system. And that is the price you'll go on paying till you waken up to the fact that the remedy's in your own hands. You've got votes – why don't you use them? Why don't you *think*?

(*Some half-hearted applause*)

A VOICE: Y'can't do without capikle!

SALLY: Going out, Ma?

MRS HARDCASTLE: Ay.

SALLY: Where to?

MRS HARDCASTLE: I'm taking Mrs Marlowe's washing. She gets that impatient.

SALLY: Look here, Mother, that's too heavy. Let me go.

(*She moves to take the basket*)

MRS HARDCASTLE: Nay, you don't. I won't have a daughter of mine carrying washing in the streets.

SALLY: Don't be daft. Give it to me.

MRS HARDCASTLE: Out of the way, Sally. Besides, I'll be right glad of a walk. (*She looks through the window*) Is that young Larry Meath spouting on the soap-box yonder?

SALLY: Maybe it is.

MRS HARDCASTLE: Maybe it is! You know well enough it is.

Politics, I suppose. Well, I've never seen much good come out of politics yet.

SALLY: Larry Meath's all right.

MRS HARDCASTLE: Aw, well, there's worse things than politics. Keeps 'em out of the pubs, any road.

(*As she is going out she meets* LARRY MEATH *at the door. He stands on one side to let her pass. He is an attractive young man, with a lean, tired face, and big eyes with a vision in them*)

LARRY: Good evening, Mrs Hardcastle.

MRS HARDCASTLE: Good evening, Mr Meath. (*With a look at* SALLY *she goes out with her washing-basket*)

LARRY: Good evening, Sally.

SALLY: Come in, lad.

(*Suddenly a* MAN *appears, points a finger at* LARRY *and shouts*)

MAN: You can't do without capikle!

(*He goes before* LARRY *can reply*)

SALLY: That's got you beat, lad.

LARRY: Hello, Sally! Were you listening?

SALLY: I can't very well do nowt else when you hold your meetings on the doorstep.

LARRY: I'm sorry. But corner of North Street always was the best place for meetings.

SALLY: Eh, I like listening to you.

LARRY: Do you really? (*Laughing*) Don't tell me I've made a convert.

SALLY: I like the way you talk. You can talk all right. But I don't know nowt— (*She corrects herself*) I mean, I don't know nothing about politics. I dunno ... It's just that I like to hear you. Here, lad, here's a cup of tea for you. Come right in. I'll bet you're thirsty after all that.

LARRY: Thanks, Sally. It's very good of you. (*He comes inside*) You know that's what's wrong with people about here. The don't know anything about politics. Make it easier if they did. The trouble is they don't seem to want to know.

SALLY: Sit down, lad. You look tired.

LARRY (*with a sigh*): Ay, it's a tough job reforming the world in Hanky Park. Don't you wish sometimes you were out of it, Sal . . . far away, somewhere else . . . ?

SALLY (*after a pause*): Aw, what's the use of feeling that way? Where can you go when you've got nowt? I was only thinking today that I've ne'er had a holiday in my life. There's not many get out of Hanky Park – except through cemet'ry gates.

LARRY: Listen. Sal, when are you coming up on the moors again?[2]

SALLY: Ee, that was champion!

LARRY: And you've never been near us since.[3]

SALLY: Eh, Larry. I ne'er thought I'd ever be going walking with you. Isn't it funny, like . . . well, y'know, us living close by all this time and . . .

LARRY: You can blame me for that. Some fellows are blind that way. But when are you coming again? They were asking for you up at the Club. (SALLY *is silent*) If you like it, why don't you come? You're welcome, you know.

SALLY: Oh, I don't like . . .

LARRY: Don't like what?

SALLY: You paying for me on the train.

LARRY (*laughing*): I can manage that.

SALLY: And the clothes them other girls wore.

LARRY: D'y'mean shorts and jerseys?

SALLY: Yes.

LARRY: Oh, there's no need to wear them if you don't like them. Besides, they don't suit everybody.

SALLY: I do like 'em. (*Indignant*) And they'd suit me, too!

LARRY: Oh, of course ... I didn't know ... I'm sorry if ...

SALLY: I should think you are! Of course, if y'think I haven't got figure for shorts and things, why don't y'say so?

LARRY: Sally, I never said ... You'd look marvellous in anything. Perhaps if we could borrow ...

SALLY: Aw, don't worry, lad, I'm only kidding. P'rhaps I'll be getting some overtime at mill,[4] then I'll be able to buy short trousers and come with you.

LARRY: That'll be great.

SALLY: But I can't promise ye fine talk like them other girls. I know nowt of Bark and Baythoven an' yon feller they call G.B.S. Is he a friend of yours?

LARRY: No, why?

SALLY: From the way they're always telling what G.B.S. said, he must have done a rare lot of talking some time or another.

LARRY: You think I talk too much, Sal?

SALLY: Nay, you mean no harm, and I like you for it. It's good talk to my way of thinking. If talking'll mek Hanky Park a better place, you'll do it.

LARRY: I wonder. It's like butting your head against a stone wall. You know, you can call those men stupid if you like, but you can't help but admire their loyalty. I mean their loyalty to a system that's made 'em what they are. They go on hoping and hoping – and every week sees another hundred of 'em out of work.[5] If they went mad and raised hell, you wouldn't blame 'em, but they're always thinking something's going to turn up. Or are they just asleep?

Gad, that's what I'm afraid of! Wakening up suddenly to find they've been done. When people wake up all of a sudden they don't act very reasonably.

SALLY: It'd be a nasty shock to wake up sudden an' find you'd been living in Hanky Park all your life.[6]

LARRY: Ach! If only we could have a fresh start all round. The kids in the gutters . . . the dirt and the smoke and the foul ugliness of it all. Oh, Sal, it gets you and it dopes you, and it eats into your heart. And it's going to be a sight worse yet, what with wage-cuts and all the rest. What's the use of talking to people – they're all too busy with their daft Irish sweeps and their coupons and their betting . . . Aw, what does it matter, anyway?

SALLY: Hey, lad, don't you get talking that way. What's come over you?

LARRY: I dunno, Sal. (*He looks at her wistfully*) I think . . . Since we've . . .

SALLY: Go on. Let's have it.

LARRY: It's . . . it's meeting you, Sal. It's made me feel kind of different about things.

SALLY: What things?

LARRY: I'm beginning to realise . . . Aw, there's something in life for me, isn't there? There's not much fun fighting for other people's lives when your own's slipping away. I tell you, Sal, I want . . .

SALLY: Want what, lad?

LARRY: It's since that day on the moors, Sal. Seeing you standing there on top of that rock with the white cloud behind you and the sun in your hair.

SALLY (*carried away and blushing happily*): It was grand, Larry! And everywhere lovely and clean.

LARRY: I dunno . . . I suppose I'm getting selfish.

SALLY: You mean? (*She is checked and disappointed*) I see.

LARRY: Oh, Sal, that's something worth living for – worth fighting for.

SALLY: I see what you mean. I'm interfering, like. If you feel that way, perhaps you'd better not come any more.

LARRY: But you don't understand, Sal. I've changed – you've changed me.

SALLY: And now you're sorry.

LARRY: No, but it makes all I'm fighting for – ideals and politics and all that – it makes it . . . well, it doesn't seem to matter like it did.

SALLY: Then, you'd best forget me standing on yon rock, and suchlike rubbish.

LARRY: You mean that, Sal? You mean you believe in what I'm trying to do?

SALLY: I don't know what you're after, proper, only to make things better.[7] But I know you're a fighter, and that's good enough for me. I don't want to stand in any chap's way. You're so different from all t'other chaps I've known. Y'don't seem to fit in with Hanky Park, some road. That's what makes me like you, and that's what makes me – afraid.

LARRY: Afraid of what?

SALLY: I dunno.

LARRY: You're a grand girl, Sal. If you knew how I felt about you . . . Aw, but what's the use?

SALLY: What's the use o' what?

LARRY: You're not laughing at me?

SALLY: No.

LARRY: I mean getting married. Buying furniture on the instalment plan. Hanky Park . . . Forty-five bob a week at Marlowe's.

SALLY: You mean you've been thinking that road?

LARRY: What d'y'take me for, Sal?

SALLY: I never thought you cared so much.

LARRY: I haven't thought of much else lately.

SALLY: An' I'm allus thinking about you, Larry. But there's some things y'can't believe in – y'know, things that make you happy, that . . .

LARRY: I know – you want to shout and tell everybody.

SALLY: Ay – or else y'want to cry.

LARRY: Lord, Sally, but I love you!

SALLY: An' I love *you*, Larry. Only don't forget you won't allus have me standing on a rock, wi' clouds, an' the sun in me hair . . .

(*He takes her in his arms and kisses her*)

LARRY: Sally!

SALLY: Why, what's wrong? There's nobody coming.

LARRY: I shouldn't be kissing you, Sal.

SALLY: Why?

LARRY: Oh, don't you see? What's the use . . . ?

SALLY: But . . . it was . . . didn't y'mean it, Larry? Didn't y'mean it?

LARRY: Of course I meant it. But let's get it straight. We both want the same thing, only . . . unless we get it straight in our minds first of all I'm no better than those other chaps. Forty-five bob a week.[8] That's all I get. And look at Marlowe's – none of us know when we're going to finish. Is it fair to you, Sal?

SALLY: I'm not a film star, Larry. I can manage as others do.

LARRY: Ay, manage to keep alive. There's something more in life than just that.

SALLY: D'y'love me?

LARRY: Would I act this way if I didn't?

SALLY: D'y'love me?

LARRY: Yes.

SALLY: Then, let's get married.

LARRY: But ...

SALLY: I'll get overtime so's we can have more money. I'll
... Oh, Larry I'd do owt for you ...!

LARRY: I know, Sal, but ...

(*She kisses him and strokes his hair*)

SALLY: Don't think so much, lad. Think about us. I want
you, and you want me. There's nowt else to it.

LARRY: Bless you, Sal! When I see you like that, with the red
in your cheeks and your eyes lit up ... you're like a
flower. (*He laughs*) A flower in Hanky Park. A rose
growing on a rubbish heap. Hanky Park ... we can't get
away from that. It's got us, it gets everybody. But when
you're near me like this, Sal, I don't seem to care. Listen,
Sal, we're going to fight it, you and me together. We'll be
different from the others. We won't go down.

SALLY: I'd want nowt else if I had you. And you can't have
everything.

LARRY: I'd have to start saving, Sal. I've no money laid by.
But if you'd wait ...

SALLY: Wait? Of course I'd wait. Oh, Larry ... (*They
embrace. Whistling is heard in the street.* HARRY *passes the
window*) Aw, there's our Harry. He would come just now.

LARRY: Right. I'll be getting along.

(HARRY *comes in from the street. He is a slightly built boy of
seventeen. He wears blue overall trousers and a jacket which
is much too small for him*)

HARRY: Hello, Larry!

LARRY: Hello! How's things, Harry?

HARRY (*grinning*): Fine! How's y'self? (*He looks at* SALLY)

LARRY: All right, thanks. Still like that job?

HARRY: Ay – it's great!

LARRY: Ah well, it's good to be young.

HARRY: I've been put on a machine – capstan-lathe. That's what I've wanted all along, and now I've got it. Have you seen new machines, Larry? By gum, they're wonderful!

LARRY: Ay, they're wonderful. They only need a lad of your years to work 'em. But they're not perfect yet, Harry.

HARRY: What do you mean, not perfect? You should see screw-cutting lathe. All as you've got to do is to shove lever over and machine does rest.

LARRY: That machine will be perfect when it turns lever for itself an' Marlowe's can be rid of young Harry Hardcastle.

HARRY (*thoughtfully*): Ay, I know that's coming. They turned another hundred fellows off this morning. But I'm not worrying. Maybe things'll take up. I could do wi' more than seventeen bob a week, though. Guh! that's a lad's pay an' I'm doin' man's work.

LARRY: That's how it is, Harry. Marlowe's want cheap labour to keep their prices down, and the apprentice racket's a good way of getting it.[9] You're in a racket, Harry, only you're in at the wrong end. Nobody'll teach you anything because there's nothing to be learnt. When you've served your time and want tradesman's pay, they'll do with you what they did with the hundred out of the machine shop this week. You'll get your cards.

SALLY (*who had been clearing up the ironing*): He should ha' gone to an office when he had chance. No short time there, an' holidays paid for.

HARRY: Aw, go on. I don't want no office. That's a tart's job. It takes a man to do with machinery.

LARRY: Well, it's a grand thing to like your work. I wish we all did. Keep young if you can, Harry.

HARRY: Young! Me? Why, I'm seventeen.

LARRY: Go on?

SALLY: Aw, he thinks he's a young Samson. I saw him feeling his muscle t'other day, like strong man at circus.

HARRY: Just you wait. I'll show you one of these days. I'm not staying in Hanky Park all me life.

(SALLY *looks at* LARRY. HARRY *looks from one to the other*)

HARRY: What's wrong?

SALLY: Nothing, lad, except that the same flea's been biting Larry and me, that's all.

HARRY: What flea?

LARRY: The Hanky Park bug, Harry. It's painful when you're young.

HARRY: I don't know what you're talking about.

LARRY: That's all right, Harry. It only bites the healthy ones.[10] Well, good night, Sal. 'Night, Harry. See you tomorrow, Sal.

(*He goes out and they bid him good night.* HARRY *is at the sink in the corner removing his jacket. He washes himself, whistling occasionally*)

HARRY: What's Larry after?

SALLY: Nowt particular.

(*She gets out a workbasket to mend some stockings*)

HARRY (*washing*): I'm right glad they've put me in machine shop. There's summat about a machine. Power – that's it. All shining new. Makes you feel grand being boss of all that power.[11] Do you feel that way yourself about machinery, Sal?

SALLY: Can't say I do.

HARRY: Aw, girls mek me sick. You never like right things. I

29

went into t'foundry today. Gosh! But that's a place, if you like. There's a whacking big crane, and it picks up twenty tons o' metal, white hot it is, like a river of fire – and they tip it in moulds, all spitting and splashing like fireworks. Fine place, Marlowe's, spite of what Larry says. Better'n a bloomin' office, any day.

SALLY: You aren't washing your neck, are you?

HARRY: Well, don't I allus do?

SALLY: Never seen you do that before.

HARRY: Gar!

SALLY: Must be going to meet a girl. Who is she?

HARRY: Girls make me sick. I tell you. Where's towel?

(*He gropes with the soap in his eyes*)

SALLY: There you are. Beside you. Does Helen Hawkins make you sick?

HARRY: She's different. I mean . . . y'know . . . *girls*.

SALLY: Oh, I see. What do you want to wear them overalls for when you've finished work?

HARRY (*hesitating*): It's . . . it's me trousers.

SALLY: What's wrong with your trousers?

HARRY: They're short 'uns.

SALLY: You mean you're still wearing them knickerbockers?

HARRY (*gloomily*): I've never had a suit o' clothes. Eh, Sal, I do wish you'd say summat to Dad about it. I'm tired of asking. And a fellow my age feels daft wearing kid's things.

SALLY: I'll try, but I don't see where the money's coming from.

HARRY: You can pay weekly at Mrs Nakkles.[12]

SALLY (*dubiously*): Your dad's suit's still at pawnshop, and we're still owing for the rent. (*She laughs*) It's a rum business!

HARRY: It's nowt to laugh at.

SALLY: You wanting long trousers and me wanting shorts.

HARRY: You in shorts! Sally, you're barmy!

SALLY: You wait. I'll show you.

(HARRY *makes a derisive noise. He is trying to fit on a collar much too large for him, before the mirror over the slopstone*)

SALLY: What you gawping at yourself for? You're worse than a girl.

HARRY (*ingratiatingly*): Would you like to make this fit me, Sal? Go on, you're a good sewer.

SALLY: What's come over you? Wearing collars?

HARRY: Go on, Sal.

SALLY: Ach! What do you think I am? I've no time to muck about with collars. I'm busy.

HARRY: Aw, Sal.

SALLY: Get Helen Hawkins to do it for you.

HARRY: I wanted you to do it, Sal. I didn't want Helen to know as Larry Meath gev it me.

SALLY: What?

HARRY: Larry gev it me. I didn't pinch it.

SALLY (*pretending unconcern*): Oh? Larry, was it? And it isn't 'gev', it's 'gave'.[13] You want to be more careful how you speak. Leave it on t'table. I'll do it later.

HARRY: Thanks, Sal. (*He looks at her curiously. Then puts on his scarf, smiling*) I tell you what, Sal, I'm having a threepenny treble every week with Sam Grundy.[14] If it comes off, I'll buy you them there shorts and owt else you're wanting. And I'll have a suit of clothes, you know, special measurement, shaped at waist like, blue serge, not one of them there reach-me-downs.

SALLY: You ought to be ashamed of yourself, spending your money on betting, and Sam Grundy, too!

HARRY: Well, Sam Grundy pays. Sky's limit with him, he says, and Bill Higgs made five quid last week on a shilling double. I'm fed up with having nowt to spend. I've no love for Sam Grundy, but I could do with some of his brass.

SALLY: Ach, the fat pig!

HARRY: Ay, y'can get away with owt when you've got brass. They say he's got women all over the shop. Down in Wales, they say, he's got a house where he keeps a woman . . .

SALLY: That'll do, lad. I know all about it. I wish he'd keep out of *my* road, that's all.

HARRY (*aghast*): Sally . . . ? You ain't . . . he ain't . . . ?

SALLY: I can manage Sam Grundy myself, thank you.

HARRY: Phew! He'd better leave you alone! It makes me feel I'd like to . . . Gosh!

SALLY: Hush!

(MRS HARDCASTLE *enters from the street. She carries a bundle which she sets down in a corner*)

MRS HARDCASTLE: Where's your dad, Sally?

SALLY: He went out.

MRS HARDCASTLE: Where?

SALLY: He didn't say. Like as not he went to Free Library to see the papers.

HARRY: Papers! They'll tell him that trade's turning the corner again. Gar! Trade's been turning corner[15] ever since I can remember. It's turned wrong corner and got lost.

MRS HARDCASTLE (*looking nervously at* SALLY): I've asked Mrs Jike to come across, Sally.

SALLY: Mrs Jike? What for, Ma?

MRS HARDCASTLE: She's holding a circle – y'know, spirits and fortune-telling. I thought she might tell us a bit.

SALLY: Oh, that fortune-telling. You know it's all nonsense.

MRS HARDCASTLE: Happen it is. And I don't really believe she talks with spirits, same as she says she does. But a bit of nonsense is a comfort sometimes.

SALLY: That means we'll have Mrs Dorbell and Mrs Bull here as well.

MRS HARDCASTLE: Well, I did say they'd be welcome. It makes it more of a party like when we're all together. Ma Jike says spirits won't come unless there's four of you . . .

HARRY: Huh! If that crowd's coming in here, I'm going out.

MRS HARDCASTLE: Harry, run upstairs and fetch that little table down. It's just the thing for spirit meetings.

HARRY: Gar! You're daft.

MRS HARDCASTLE: Go on, quick! (*He goes out on the right*) Let's hope your dad stays out a bit. He doesn't like Mrs Jike an' her friends. (*She washes some plates at the slopstone*) Mrs Jike was saying that you and Larry Meath—

SALLY: Interferin' cat! Tell her to mind her own business.

MRS HARDCASTLE: I don't think she meant anything. She just said as how she'd seen him. Ay, he's a nice young man is that Mr Meath. I do like him, I do.

SALLY (*eagerly*): Do you really, Ma?

MRS HARDCASTLE: I do. I reckon he's a genkleman, and a credit to the neighbourhood, and never heed what folks say about Labour[16] men.

SALLY: Ay, Ma. That Sunday we went up on the moors. We had a grand time. Over mountains as high as you never saw. And he knows the names of all the birds.

MRS HARDCASTLE: Eh, ain't that nice, now? Though I can't see as it's much good knowing names of all the birds.

SALLY: Better than knowing names of horses.

MRS HARDCASTLE: Ay, eddication's like that. Knowing a lot of things as don't really matter.

SALLY: And he paid me fare. Oh, I was in a stew when I heard the others say fare was two shillings and me with only tenpence in me purse. I never knew it'd be so much. But I think he knew how I was fixed, 'cos when I got all bothered he smiled – you know how he smiles, Ma – well, he smiled like that and said he'd got tickets for both of us and that was all right. Though he said it different . . . he wouldn't have done that if he hadn't . . . didn't . . .

MRS HARDCASTLE: That's true. When I was a lass it was took for granted that when a lad paid for you to places he meant summat serious.

SALLY: There was a girl in party that made herself free wi' him. She was trying to rile me, I know. But he took no notice of *her* much, and he kept with me all the while . . . (*She sighs*) Ah, I love way he talks. An' he's so . . . so . . . nice, if you know what I mean.

MRS HARDCASTLE: I know.

SALLY: I never enjoyed meself so much in all me life.

MRS HARDCASTLE: Did he ask you to go again?

SALLY: Yes. He asked me again, just now. An' . . . (*She checks herself*)

MRS HARDCASTLE: What was you goin' to say?

SALLY: Nowt – only I hope I get some overtime at mill.

MRS HARDCASTLE: What for?

SALLY: So's I can get a rig-out like rest of the girls. I felt proper out of it against them and their heavy boots and jerseys and short trousers.

MRS HARDCASTLE: Eee . . . ! Short trousers? Our Sally . . . ?

SALLY: They all wear shorts up on the moors.

MRS HARDCASTLE: You're not thinking . . . ?

SALLY: 'Course I am.

MRS HARDCASTLE: Do you think your father'd like you to be dressed like that, Sal?

SALLY: Aw, who cares what he thinks? I'll buy 'em an' I'll wear 'em. Let him mind his own business.

MRS HARDCASTLE: Once your character was as good as gone when you wore short skirts. But short trousers . . . *my!*

(MR HARDCASTLE *enters from the street. He is a thickset miner, with a square-set reliable face, and hair and mous-tache turning grey*)

Drat it! Here's your father.

HARDCASTLE (*hanging up his cap behind the door*): What's to do, Ma? (*He goes over to the fire filling his pipe*)

MRS HARDCASTLE: Thought you were going to be out tonight, Henry.

HARDCASTLE: I've changed me mind. That's about all I have to change.

MRS HARDCASTLE: You won't find it very nice with all them clothes hanging up to dry.

HARDCASTLE: All right, Ma. Don't you worry about me. Happen I'll go out again soon.

MRS HARDCASTLE (*relieved*): Ah.

(HARRY *enters with table*)

HARRY: Here you are, Ma.

HARDCASTLE: What's Harry doing with yon table?

MRS HARDCASTLE: That? Oh, Mrs Jike's coming in.

HARDCASTLE: Ach! I thought you were going to take it to pawnshop.

(HARRY *makes signs to* SALLY)

HARRY: Go on, Sal. Ask him now.

SALLY: No, lad. Not now.

(SALLY *picks up her sewing and goes out.* HARDCASTLE *takes out a crumpled newspaper and reads it*)

HARRY: Ma?

MRS HARDCASTLE: Yes?

HARRY: When am I going t'have that there new suit?

MRS HARDCASTLE (*sighing*): Eh, lad, what can I do? Y'know Sal's not drawing much, and your pa's only on three days, and ain't sure of that . . .

HARRY: I know, Ma. But I've never had a proper suit. And me nearly eighteen.

MRS HARDCASTLE: You're pa's tired now.

HARRY: Yes, but I'm ashamed to go out of a Sunday in these. An' I can't wear little trousers like as if I was a kid. Look at Bill Lindsay and the others. They can have 'em. Why can't I?

MRS HARDCASTLE: They get 'um from Good Samaritan Clothing Club, Harry. You know your dad don't like weekly payments. (*They both look hopefully at* HARD-CASTLE) Leave him be. He's tired.

HARRY: But I don't see . . .

(HARDCASTLE *removes his pipe from his mouth and spits into the fire*)

HARDCASTLE: You'll have to make do with what you've got, lad. It's taking us all our time to live. You'll get one when things buck up.[17]

HARRY (*petulant*): When things buck up! Huh!

HARDCASTLE: It's all very well talking that way. But trade's turning the corner. Paper says so.

HARRY: Aw, I know I'm ashamed to turn the corner in these trousers.

MRS HARDCASTLE: Now, Harry, let your father be.

HARRY: Why can't I have one through the Good Samaritan like the others?

HARDCASTLE (*sternly*): I'll tell you for why. Because I'm not shoving no bloomin' millstone of weekly payments round me neck. What we can't pay for cash down we'll do bout.[18] See?

HARRY: But the others do it. And here I am working full time and ain't got nowt to go out in of weekends.

HARDCASTLE: Aaach! I've worked all me bloomin' life, lad, an' what've *I* got? All me bloomin' clothes in pawn to get food to eat. Don't you set me off, now! Don't you set me off!

MRS HARDCASTLE (*pleading*): Now, Harry, please . . .

HARRY (*angry and almost tearful*): Well, I'm sick of it all, I can tell you. Nowt to spend and nowt to wear and me working full time. *Man's* work, that's what I do.[19] And givin' up all I earn, bar a shilling spends.

(HARDCASTLE *flings down his newspaper and jumps up blazing*)

HARDCASTLE: God Almighty! This is a fine life, this is! I come home to rest and what do I get? If it ain't you, it's Sally. Blimey, man, do you think blasted money grows on trees?

MRS HARDCASTLE: Well, the lad's right, Henry. He ain't fit to be seen in the street.

HARDCASTLE: Worked every hour God sent, every day of me life. And what have I to show for it? Every blasted day, every blasted hour and worse off than when I was first wed.

MRS HARDCASTLE: It's a lot of brass, Harry. Three pounds.

HARDCASTLE: Huh! Three pounds!

MRS HARDCASTLE: You see you pay three bob poundage[20] for the check,[21] and three bob a week for twenty weeks.

HARRY: Can't go out weekdays except in me overalls. And I've to stay in all of Sunday with everybody asking me why don't I come out . . .

HARDCASTLE: Oh, missis, for God's sake get him that blasted suit. G'blind owd Riley, I'm fair sick o' it all, I am!

HARRY (*fervently*): Oh, thanks, Dad, thanks . . . !

MRS HARDCASTLE: But, Henry, how are we goin' to . . . ?

HARDCASTLE: We'll have to manage some road.

MRS HARDCASTLE: Three bob a week . . .

HARRY: Can I go now, Ma, to the Good Samaritan?

HARDCASTLE: Ay, go as quick as you can before I change me mind.

HARRY (*all smiles*): Oo heck! You don't know how I feel about it. I'm off. S'long!

(*He picks up his cap and darts out*)

MRS HARDCASTLE: Henry . . .

HARDCASTLE: Well?

MRS HARDCASTLE: Do you think you ought to have given in?

HARDCASTLE: What the hell could I do? Lad's right. If I'd had any sense, I'd have said 'No'. But I never did have any sense. Besides, he ain't fit to be seen.

MRS HARDCASTLE: I don't know how we're going to pay.

HARDCASTLE: Summat else'll have to go, that's all. We'll start with this.

(*He knocks out his pipe, and puts it carefully into one of the ornaments on the mantelshelf*)

MRS HARDCASTLE: Not your pipe, Henry. You can't do without your pipe.

HARDCASTLE: Can't I? We'll see about that.

MRS HARDCASTLE: Makes y'that narky when you don't have tobacco.

HARDCASTLE: Well, I'll just have to be narky, then. Though I can't feel much worse than I do now.

(*He puts on his cap*)

MRS HARDCASTLE: Are you going out?

HARDCASTLE: Yes.

MRS HARDCASTLE: Where are you going?

HARDCASTLE: I'm going t'take out me brains and put 'em in cold water.

MRS HARDCASTLE: You're not angry with me, Henry?

HARDCASTLE: With you? No.

MRS HARDCASTLE: Nor Harry?

HARDCASTLE: Harry? (*He laughs*) Nay, he's a good lad.

MRS HARDCASTLE: Then, who are you angry with?[22]

HARDCASTLE: I don't rightly know. By God, I'd give 'em a piece of me mind.

(*He goes out.* MRS HARDCASTLE *fills the kettle and puts it on the fire.* SALLY *comes in*)

SALLY: Has Dad gone out?

MRS HARDCASTLE: Yes.

SALLY: Was there a row?

MRS HARDCASTLE: I've seen worse. Your dad let himself go, but Harry got his trousers in the end. He's gone to Good Samaritan about it now.

SALLY: I suppose I'll have to get overtime at mill now and no mistake. And it's goodbye to them shorts of mine.

MRS HARDCASTLE: Ah, well, I can't say as I'm going to fret much about that. There'd be too much talk in North Street with you walking about half-naked.

SALLY: I'd do it to give 'em summat to talk about. Gosh! I would!

MRS HARDCASTLE: Now, then, Sally. Don't talk that way. Ee, I'd be glad if you could settle down with a young man like Larry Meath. There's so many of the wrong sort knocking about these days.

SALLY: Um. Chance is a fine thing.

MRS HARDCASTLE: Has he never asked you?

SALLY: He has – and he hasn't. But I've asked *him*, though.

MRS HARDCASTLE (*shocked*): Sally!

SALLY: Well, why not? A woman usually asks a man some road or another, though she doesn't allus do it with her tongue. I'm one for plain speaking.

MRS HARDCASTLE: You don't mean to say you asked him to marry you?

SALLY: I did.

MRS HARDCASTLE: Eh, Sally, it's not respectable. I *am* ashamed of you. (*Eagerly*) What did he say?

SALLY: He said we'd have to wait. And he's saving up.

MRS HARDCASTLE: I wonder what the end of it all'll be. That's where Mrs Jike can help us, maybe.

SALLY: Oh, that kind of thing's daft!

MRS HARDCASTLE: It ain't daft at all. Ma Jike tells fortunes true. She warned Mrs Dorbell when her Willie was going to die, though I must say his cough was summat awful at the time. (*There is a knock on the door*) There's Mrs Jike, now. (*Calling*) Come in, Mrs Jike!

(SALLY *opens the door.* MRS JIKE *is a tiny woman with a man's cap and late-Victorian bodice and skirt. She talks with a cockney accent, being a 'transplanted sprig of London Pride from Whitechapel'. She is followed by* MRS DORBELL, *a beshawled ancient woman with a dewdrop at the end of her hooked prominent nose.* MRS JIKE *carries a concertina under her shawl. They come inside)*

MRS JIKE: Are you in, missis?

MRS DORBELL: 'Course she's in – can't you see her?

MRS HARDCASTLE: Come in, everybody. Good evening, Mrs Dorbell, and you, Mrs Jike. Where's Mrs Bull?

MRS JIKE: We left her having an argument with a lady.

(MRS BULL *appears in the doorway, carrying on a spirited conversation with an unseen antagonist)*

MRS BULL: Go on with you! You trombone-playing old faggot. Give your husband his trousers back! Yah! If he'd any guts, he'd knock your face in.

A VOICE: Pay your debts! Pay your debts, says me, and stare the world in the face!

MRS BULL: Yah! You bleeding little gutter-rat! Ay, an' take y'r face inside, you're blocking traffic in the street! (*With this parting shot she slams the door)* I'll teach her to argue with me. Good evening, Sarah. That Mrs Scodger's getting a bit above hersel'.

MRS HARDCASTLE: Now, sit down, everybody, and make yourselves at home.

MRS JIKE (*to* SALLY): Well, dearie! I saw you walking out with Mr Meath.

MRS BULL: Ay, Larry Meath's a gradely lad, and that lass of thine's lucky to have gotten him. He ain't of the strongest, though, and he'd do better if he took care of that cough o' his. I don't like it, Sally. I expects it's consumption. Clever 'uns allus die that road.

MRS DORBELL: It's all this politician-is-ing he's been doing lately. I wouldn't like any daughter of mine to marry a Bolshy. Look what women've done in Russia. Broken up the home life, and nationalising of women. I wouldn't have nobody nationalising me.

MRS BULL: Shouldn't think there's many as would want to.

MRS JIKE: Here you are, gels. Have a pinch of Bird's Eye.[23] It'll do you good.

(*Her snuff-box is handed to* MRS BULL *and* MRS DORBELL)

MRS HARDCASTLE: I'm brewin' a pot o' tea. It'll be ready in a minute. How are you, Mrs Bull? I haven't seen you much lately.

MRS BULL: Trade's bad.

MRS HARDCASTLE: I'm sorry. Sally, get them cups out. How's that, Mrs Bull?

MRS BULL: Yah . . . I don't know what's come over folk these days. I remember time when never a day hardly passed without there was a confinement or a laying-out to be done. Young 'uns ain't having childer as they should. And them as die are bin' laid out by them as they belong to, which weren't considered respectable in th'owld days. When I was a gel a 'ooman wasn't a 'ooman till she'd been in childbed ten times not counting miscarriages. Aach! How do they expect a body to make a livin' when childer goin' t'school know more about things than we do after we'd been married years?

MRS JIKE: That's just it.

MRS DORBELL: Thing's ain't been the same since genklefolk left th'owld Road.[24] In *them* days a body could allus depend on summat new to pawn. Eh, ay, I remember when I was a likkle girl how my owld ma – God rest her soul in peace (*she crosses herself*) – how my owld ma used to fetch us all in out of street when charity ladies came round in their kerridges hinquirin' for them as was hard up. 'Come on now,' she used to say. 'Off'n with them pinnies and your clogs and stockings.' Then she'd send us out in street and ladies'd take us names for a new rig-out. Eh, many a bright shilling they fetched at pawnshop. You don't see nowt like that nowadays. If you've got nowt you get nowt and nobody cares. Eh, ay, if my owld ma was alive to see things today she'd turn over in her grave, that she would.

MRS JIKE: The world's never been the same since the old Queen died.

MRS BULL: What Queen do you mean, Mrs Jike?

MRS JIKE: Why, Queen Victoria, of course. When I used to live in London – that was the time. Look at 'em now. I see in me paper this morning as they're havin' boxing matches in the 'Elbert 'All! Eh, the old Queen'd give 'em snuff if she were alive. She would that! Thank you kindly, Mrs Hardcastle. Would any lady care to have a drop of this in her tea?

(*She produces a flat bottle of gin from her stocking.* MRS BULL *and* MRS DORBELL *accept.* SALLY *sits well apart from the others darning socks*)

MRS DORBELL: Thank you, Mrs Jike. I don't mind if I do. How's your rheumatic, Mrs Bull?

MRS BULL: I'd be all right only for a twinge now and again. But I don't worry none. There's a rare lot up in the cemetery as'd be glad of a twinge or two.

MRS JIKE (*looking at the bottle*): 'Ere! Somebody's done herself well. You may be alcoholic, Mrs Dorbell, but y'might have the manners of a lady.

MRS HARDCASTLE: Now, now. I thought as y'might like to hold a circle, Mrs Jike. That's why I brought out table.

MRS JIKE: Well, that all depends on the spirits, doesn't it?

MRS DORBELL (*bursting into song*): 'We'll laugh an' we'll sing an' we'll drive away care, I've enough for meself an' a little bit to spare. If a nice young man should ride my way, Oo-ow, I'll make him welcome as the flowers in May!'

MRS BULL (*laughing loudly*): That's it – a bit o' music. When I hear a bit of music I don't know meself.

MRS DORBELL: Play us a tune, Mrs Jike.

MRS JIKE (*producing her concertina*): 'Ere, steady on! Not that sort o' music. You'll drive the spirits away. Turn the lamp down low, dearie. All round the table now. All hands on table-top. Only just your finger-ends. (*She plays a hymn tune, in which they join lugubriously. At the end she clears her throat, takes a drink from her bottle, and addresses the shadows in the room*) Is the spirits present here tonight? Answer 'three' for 'yes' and 'two' for 'no'. (*Three bumps come from somewhere under the table*) Ah! They're present. Now, hush! Has anybody got anythink to ask the spirits about?

MRS DORBELL: Ya. Mrs Nakkles's got a ticket in Irish Sweep and her wants me to go shares. Ask spirits if I do will ticket draw a horse?

MRS JIKE: Will Mrs Nakkles's ticket draw a horse?

(*Two bumps*)

MRS DORBELL: Right. And thank you. Her can keep her owld ticket. I want none of it.

MRS JIKE: Hush, Mrs Dorbell, hush. Spirits don't like too much talking. Any more questions?

MRS BULL: Is Jack Tuttle there? (*Three bumps*) Eh, Jack lad, are you there? Well, hark to me. When I laid thee out, lad, I found half a crown in thy pocket an' I was hard up so I took it. I know tha wouldna need it where tha's gone, an' I'm only telling you this so's you'd not think I'd pinched it. How do you find things where tha art, Jack? Is it owt like tha thowt it'd be? (*Three bumps*) Eh, lad, forgive me for sayin' it, but it took thee a long time to go. For years an' years I was expecting you going every day.

MRS JIKE: Ask questions, Mrs Bull. The spirits don't like y'to be familiar.

SALLY (*on the other side of the room*): Oh, stop it! I never heard anything so daft in me life.

MRS JIKE: Eh, what? Now you've done it! They've gorn!

SALLY: I think you're an old twister, Mrs Jike.

MRS JIKE: Ow, am I? I like that!

MRS BULL: Go on, Sally lass. It's only a bit o' fun and it costs nowt.

MRS DORBELL: Anyway, I'd have bought shares of ticket if spirits had said it was going to draw horse, fun or no fun. Ee! Fancy me winning thirty thousand quid! I'd buy meself fur coat an' . . .

MRS BULL: Ay, and I'd be laying you out in a month, drunk to death, fur coat and all.

MRS DORBELL: I'd risk it. I'd have a good time once, anyway!

MRS HARDCASTLE: I'd love Sally to have her fortune told, Mrs Jike, spite of what she says.

MRS JIKE (*sniffing*): Can't say as I'll do it for an antiskeptic.

MRS HARDCASTLE: Aw, come on, Mrs Jike. Sally meant no harm.

SALLY: I don't want me fortune told.

MRS HARDCASTLE: Now, Sally, just to please me.

MRS JIKE: Remember I ain't responsible. Will you 'ave cards or tea-leaves?

MRS DORBELL: Make it tea-leaves. It's more exciting when you go seeing things in the future, the way you do.

MRS JIKE: Very well. (*She takes up Sally's cup*) Strike me pink! Look at that!

MRS DORBELL: What is it?

MRS JIKE: Money! Lot's o' money!

MRS DORBELL: Oo!

MRS BULL: Ay, in the bank.

MRS JIKE: Hush! I see two men . . . one's thin and dark. Do you know a thin dark man?

(SALLY *does not answer*)

MRS HARDCASTLE: Ay, that'll be Larry Meath.

MRS JIKE: The other's a fat man. Be on your guard. 'E means danger. Oo! And money, more money . . .

MRS DORBELL: Yus, and then what?

MRS JIKE: Now I'm seeing things. Right through the bottom of the tea-cup I'm seeing, into the future. It's all dark . . . darkness all round you . . . I see Sally 'Ardcastle and the thin little bloke. They're trying to get to the light, but down they go into the darkness . . . I can't see no more . . . it's getting darker an' darker . . . Ow!

(*She screams suddenly*)

MRS HARDCASTLE: What is it? Oh, what is it?

MRS JIKE: All red! Like blood . . .

SALLY: Stop it! Do you hear, you old fool? Stop it!

(*She turns up the light*)

MRS BULL: Now see what you've done. You've frightened the lass. You didn't ought to do that.

SALLY: Get outside, all the lot of you!

MRS HARDCASTLE: Sally!

SALLY: Yes, Ma. I mean it. You ought to be ashamed of yourself bringing 'um in here. Go on, get out! If you don't go, I'll put you out! Whole damned pack of you.

MRS JIKE: I warned you!

SALLY: You dirty owld scut! Do you think I believe a word you've said?

MRS JIKE: Ow? So that's how you feel, is it? Come along, Mrs Dorbell.

(*She goes out*)

MRS DORBELL: And I was expecting to have mine told, too.

MRS BULL: I can tell it, lass. Tha'll keep on drawing thy owld-age pension, and then tha'll dee, an I'll lay thee out and parish'll bury you. Come on, we aren't wanted.

MRS DORBELL: Good night, Mrs Hardcastle, I'm sorry y'daughter was took that way.

(*She follows* MRS JIKE *into the street*)

MRS BULL: Good night. Eh, Sal, lass. Take no notice of what Mrs Jike says. It's a bit o' fun. Good night, Sarah.

(*She goes out.* SALLY *bangs the door after her*)

SALLY: There! And good riddance, too!

MRS HARDCASTLE (*almost in tears*): Sally! What've you done?

SALLY: I've turned 'em out. And about time, too.

MRS HARDCASTLE: But, Sally ... you've shamed me ... they're me friends. What'll they think of me?

SALLY: Friends? Those our friends? It's us that's shamed, Ma, by havin' owt to do with 'em.

MRS HARDCASTLE: Sally! You're not gettin' notions, are you?

SALLY: Yes, I am getting notions. It's about time some of us in Hanky Park *started* getting notions. You call 'em your friends, that pack o' dirty owld women? Oh, I'm not blaming 'em – that's what Hanky Park's done for 'em. It's what it does for all the women.[25] It's what it'll do to you, Ma ... yes, it will! ... and me too! We'll all go t'same road – poverty and pawnshops and dirt and drink!

Well, I'm not going that road, and neither are you, if I can help it. I'm going to fight it – me and Larry's goin' to fight it – an' I'm starting *now*.

MRS HARDCASTLE: You can't, Sally, you can't. I've tried and you can't . . .

SALLY: Can't you? We'll see about that!

MRS HARDCASTLE: You're hard, Sally. You're like all the young 'uns, you're hard.

SALLY: Ay, I'm hard . . . and by God you need to be.

CURTAIN

ACT II

SCENE 1[26]

An alley in Hanky Park. In the brick wall facing us is the entrance to a narrow passage. A street-lamp on a bracket. A dustbin stands against the wall, and there are a few tattered posters, giving racing news and offering large cash prizes. It is night, and the lamp is lighted. We hear the mournful note of a ship's siren on the Ship Canal.

A POLICEMAN *is standing beside the entrance to the passage. A man passes by reading an evening paper.*

POLICEMAN: Good night, Charlie.

CHARLIE: Hello! Is that you, Joe? Looks like we'll have more rain.

POLICEMAN: Ay. More rain, more rest. Heigh, ho!

CHARLIE: No rest for the wicked, lad, 'cept them as is bobbies, and they never do nowt else. I don't know how some folks . . .

POLICEMAN: I know, Charlie . . . I know. I know all about it.

CHARLIE: Well, there's one thing I'd like to know if tha knows all about it – how thee and thy mates have cheek to hold hand out for wages just for standing about in street? No wonder folks call it a bobby's job.

POLICEMAN: Ay, you've a lot to learn. A police officer gets a bird's-eye view, as you might say.

CHARLIE: You ain't much of a bloomin' bird, to look at you.

POLICEMAN: We see life as it is – in the raw. Take people in this town. Have you ever seen a lot of maggots squirming in tin, same as fishers have for bait on canal bank?

CHARLIE: Maggots in a tin! Huh!

POLICEMAN: That's how I see the people in Hanky Park. All

in the same tin together, wriggling and fighting, and none of 'em knows how they got in, nor how they're going to get out. That's philosophy, that is.

CHARLIE: Seems a pity you've all that time for thinking if it takes you that road.

POLICEMAN: Mind you, I don't say as I'd let thinking interfere with the performance of duty. Philosophy's all right s'long as you keep it in its place. Once it gets to your head there's no telling what might happen.

CHARLIE: Here, want a tip for two-thirty t'morrow?

POLICEMAN: Officially, no. But there's no harm in knowing. What is it?

CHARLIE: 'Dusty Carpet.' You put your money on it. It'll want some beating. Good night, Joe.

(CHARLIE *goes quickly*)

POLICEMAN: 'Night, Charlie. I'll bear it in mind.

(*The* POLICEMAN *goes in the opposite direction, thinking hard. As soon as he has gone* HARRY *pops round the corner of the passage. With him is* HELEN HAWKINS, *a girl of about sixteen*)

HELEN: Have they gone?

HARRY: Yes. And it's time I was going, too.

HELEN: Oh, Harry, let's not fall out.[27]

HARRY: What do you mean? *Us* fall out? Huh! I like that!

HELEN: Oh, Harry, I never meant . . .

HARRY: Oh, that's all right. You're allus making a fuss. Girls make me sick as a rule, but you're not so bad.

HELEN (*eagerly*): Do you mean that, Harry? Do you mean it?

HARRY: Do I mean what?

HELEN: That I'm not so bad.

HARRY (*lighting a cigarette end*): Um. But, don't forget, I'm not walking out regular. Not yet.

HELEN (*disappointed*): Oh ... I dunno what's come over you lately, Harry.

HARRY: What do you mean?

HELEN: I mean – I thought you and me were ...

HARRY: Well, we are in a way, aren't we? But I can't allus be ... you see, there's the other chaps. I don't like 'em saying things.

HELEN: What sort of things?

HARRY: Aw, just – things.

HELEN: Never heed what they say. Oh, Harry, we could be ... you know. I've allus liked you best of everybody, and ... oh, well, you're different from the other lot.

HARRY: Aw, the lads are all right. It's like this, you see. I like you, too. Yes, I do, really, no kidding. But ... well, I don't want to go out regular with nobody yet. I ... Oh, I dunno, Helen, I want to do things first.

HELEN: What like?

HARRY: Big things. Make money, or summat. Gosh, I wish I were a footballer or a boxer, or summat like that.

HELEN: Harry, I do love ye ... I do really.

HARRY: Do you, Helen? Thanks. (*But he puts his arm round her*) You see, Helen, it troubles me, having nowt to spend on you. It's rotten – kids get more to spend than me. Older you grow, more work you do and less money you get to spend. Why, when I first started at Marlowe's, what with money I got for brewing tea and running errands – I got twice as much then as what I do now. And me on a machine ... Gar!

HELEN: Oh, ne'er mind about money. I don't want nowt, Harry. Only you.

HARRY: Well, let me get out of me time,[28] an' on full money.
I'll show you . . . I'll find a job . . .

HELEN: Would y'rather be with street-corner lads than here
with me? Would you? Would you, Harry . . . ?

HARRY: No fear.

HELEN: Oh, Harry!

HARRY: You know, Helen, you aren't bad-looking.

HELEN (*eagerly*): Aren't I, Harry?

HARRY: You're not exactly . . . well, you aren't Greta Garbo.
But you'll do. (*He kisses her*) There! I'm not the sort that
does that for nowt.

HELEN: Eh, Harry, y'do make me happy.

HARRY: Rum place for being happy, isn't it? Back entry in
Hanky Park. I allus used t'think of love like on the
Pictures, with moonlight and trees.

HELEN: I reckon love's same the world over. Though I could
do with moonlight and trees better'n brick walls and
chimney stacks. But it doesn't matter, does it, Harry?

HARRY (*wistfully*): No . . . it doesn't really matter.

HELEN (*drawing his face to hers*): It's you and me.

HARRY: Ay, that's it, Helen. Me and you. It's strange like,
but that's how it is. (*A train rumbles and puffs along a
neighbouring viaduct*) Look at yon. I've never been on the
train in me life.

HELEN: No more have I.

(*They watch it go*)

HARRY: I wish I had more money just so's we could have a
bit more fun. I'd like to be able to take you and me away
for a holiday.

HELEN: Oo, you can't do that!

HARRY: Just you wait. You don't know what I'm doing on
the quiet.

HELEN: What? Not – stealing?

HARRY: Me – no! One of these days I'll make more money than you ever saw.

HELEN: What is it?

HARRY: Well, I'm having a threepenny treble every week with Sam Grundy.

HELEN: What's a threepenny treble?

HARRY: Well, it's this way. You put threepence on a horse, whatever you fancy, of course, and if horse wins, what you've made you play on another horse, and any winnings from that you play on another.

HELEN: You mean three horses have got to win?

HARRY: Ay.

HELEN: Isn't it very difficult?

HARRY: To some it is. You got to be a student of form. But Bill Higgs won five pounds on a shilling double, so I'm hoping.

HELEN: Five pounds!

HARRY (*eagerly*): You see, I put me threepence on Columbus. That's a twenty-to-one chance. Then there's Jackdaw in the three o'clock, that's another twenty-to-one, and I'm playing it all on Tea Rose in the three-thirty. It's exciting, you know. When I look in the paper tomorrow, it'll be in the stop-press. I stand to win – ooh – I don't know how much, and I can't lose more'n threepence, you see. Oh, Helen, if I could make some money, there's things we could do, you and me . . .

(*The light has faded. A siren moans dismally on the Ship Canal. Out of the darkness comes the voice of the paper-boy calling, 'News Chroniker! Three o'clock winner. Racing Special. Evenin' News! Evenin' Chroniker! News Chroniker!' The light returns, and now it is the daylight of late afternoon. A group of men and women arrive during the scene. Another man buys a paper, forming a second group.* MRS BULL *appears with* MRS DORBELL)

MRS BULL: ... Ay, an' he's had a threepenny treble every week for years. This is the first time it's ever come off.

MRS DORBELL: Twenty-two quid for threepence!

MRS BULL: Ay, what do you think of that? He ain't twenty year old yet, neither, not by a long way.

A MAN: Who is it, Mrs Bull?

MRS BULL: Harry Hardcastle. Him as lives at Number Seventeen.

MRS DORBELL: Twenty-two quid for threepence! Yah! Some hopes!

MRS BULL (*talking well-off*): Mrs Dorbell, I ain't in the habit of havin' me word doubted, especially by one of me neighbours.

(*The interest begins to shift to* MRS BULL's *group*)

A MAN: Are you sure it's true?

VOICES: What's up? Who is it? Harry Hardcastle! Etc.

MRS BULL: True? It's true as God's above. Threepence win on a twenty-to-one chance, that's five an' three – all on Jackdaw as won three o'clock at twenty to one. That made it over five quid, and he played it all on Tea Rose in three-thirty an' *that* came up at three to one. What do you think of that?

A MAN: Blimey! I could do with that meself. Some people have all the ruddy luck!

VOICES: Twenty-two quid, I tell ye! Harry Hardcastle. Threepenny treble ... etc., etc.

MRS BULL: Ay – young Harry Hardcastle. Him as lives in North Street.

MRS DORBELL: That's all very well, but will Sam Grundy pay him?

A MAN: Ay, will Sam Grundy pay up?

MRS BULL: Ah, now you're askin' summat. That's what we're all here to see. If he does, then Sam Grundy gets all my bets in future, you bet he will.

MRS DORBELL: Sam Grundy should be here by now. It looks kind of suspicious. Huh! I bet he don't pay up.

A VOICE: Hey! There's the lad! Harry Hardcastle!

(*There is considerable excitement as* HARRY *appears, newspaper in hand*)

VOICES: Good old Harry! He's got a treble home! *Twenty-two quid!* . . . Congratulations, Harry. You'll be going to t'Rivy-eera now . . .

MRS BULL (*taking his arm*): Eh, Harry lad, who'd have thought it! I hope Sam Grundy pays up.

HARRY: Ay, so do I.

A MAN: Here, lend us y'paper. Sky's limit with him, he says. Thee look after thy money.

HARRY: I will that.

MRS BULL: And you'll stand us a bottle of gin, won't you, Harry?

(SALLY *appears at the edge of the crowd*)

MRS DORBELL: There's some bookies what won't pay more than five pounds. And, if you ask me, this here sky's-the-limit business is all a bit of bluff. I wouldn't give much for your chances, lad.

(HARRY *has broken away and joined* SALLY. *The crowd begins to surge round the entry at the back*)

SALLY: Is it true, Harry?

HARRY: Ay, I think so. Twenty-two quid!

SALLY: That's fine, lad.

HARRY: I'll be able to pay for that new suit of mine now, and to hell with weekly payments.

SALLY: Now, don't go being soft with all that brass.

MRS BULL (*who is hovering*): That's what I were just telling him.

SALLY: You keep out of this!

MRS BULL (*moving away*): All right, Sally Hardcastle. I won't rob you of your lawful pickings. Though I warn you there's nowt like brass for breaking up a fambly.

HARRY (*to* SALLY): Take no notice. I say, Sal, you can have them shorts and things as soon as you like.

SALLY: No, it's your money.

HARRY: Go on, I promised you, and you've got to have 'em.

SALLY: Thanks, Harry.

(*The crowd is shouting excitedly*)

VOICES: Come on, Sam! We want Sam!

A MAN (*turning to* HARRY): Hey, lad, here's Sam Grundy.

VOICE OF CHARLIE (*in the entry*): Make way there! Way for Sam Grundy!

VOICES: Here he is! etc.

(*A lane opens in the crowd and Sam Grundy swaggers through. He is a small fat man, with beady eyes and an apoplectic complexion. His thumbs are usually in his waistcoat arm-holes, and his huge gold watch-chain and diamond ring suggest great prosperity. He wears spats, and a billycock tilted at the back of his head*)

SAM: Well? Where's Harry Hardcastle? (HARRY *is pushed forward to meet* SAM) So that's him, is it? Not much to look at, is he? (*Roars of obsequious laughter*) Well, lad, so you thought y'd break bank, eh? (*More laughter.* HARRY *grins sheepishly*) Now, young fellow me lad, you know some bookies have a limit. You know that, don't you, eh?

MRS DORBELL: There you are! Didn't I tell you? Garn, pay him. You're like all the rest.

(*There is a faint groan of dismay*)

SAM (*waving his hand*): Half a mo', half a mo'! I haven't finished yet. Now, there's fellers as calls themselves bookies as'd only pay you a fiver on your bet and no more. You know that, don't you?

HARRY: I do.

SAM: Well me lad, that ain't the way of honest Sam Grundy. Sam Grundy pays up – that's me! (*He removes his hat with a flourish. Roars of applause and shouts of 'Good owd Sam!' etc.*) Charlie, fetch a chair! Nay, fetch two chairs. We're going to do this thing proper and all square and fair and above board. (CHARLIE *places the chairs at the mouth of the entry.* SAM *mounts one carefully*) Now, listen to me, ladies and gentlemen. Honest Sam's gotta motter, an' that motter is 'Sky's the limit'. Don't forget it, sky's the limit with honest Sam Grundy. This here young feller me lad . . . stand up alongside of me, son, and let's have a look at you. Now, you had a bet with me, didn't you, lad? (HARRY *blushes and nods*) How much were it?

HARRY (*muttering*): Threepence.

SAM: Aw, now, lad, come on! There's nowt to be ashamed on. There ain't nobody here as wouldn't give ten pounds to be in your shoes. Eh, what d'y'say? (*Tumult, which* SAM *quells by holding up a fat hand*) Now, lad, speak up. How much were the bet? Turn to the crowd lad, turn to the crowd.

HARRY (*shouting*): Threepence!

SAM: And how much do you reckon to draw for threepence? (*To the crowd*) Listen to this, now, listen to this.

HARRY (*loudly*): Twenty-two quid!

(*A universal hubbub.* SAM *lights a cigar*)

SAM: Twenty-two quid for threepence. How many bookies'd pay out that much? Eh – how many? Well, you all know honest Sam's motter. What is it, Harry? Hey, Charlie . . . (CHARLIE *passes up a handful of notes*) What's Honest Sam's motter, Harry? And remember people at back. Let 'em hear you!

HARRY (*bawling*): Sky's the limit!

SAM: Hold out your cap, Harry, lad. Five, ten, fifteen, twenty – and two. Twenty-two quid. That's Honest Sam for you, ladies and gents. What can't speak can't lie.

MRS JIKE: What about his stake money?

(SAM *counts three pennies into the cap, the crowd counting aloud in unison*)

SAM (*aside to* HARRY): Ain't that your sister, young Sal? Don't forget to give her a couple of quid. Tell her I said so. And now, ladies and gents – (HARRY *frowns at* SAM *and gets down. He forces his way through the admiring crowd, and goes to* SALLY. SAM *speaks on*) doesn't that prove as I'm the man for your little commissions. Support Sam Grundy, the old firm, and take a threepenny treble every week. Take one for the wife and little 'uns, too. There's nowt like it. Better'n insurance any day. Yes, sir. Charlie, give this genkleman a slip. There you are ladies and gents, that's the way to make money quick. Risk a bit and gain a lot. That's the way the money's made in this world. Honest Sam, the old firm . . . (CHARLIE *is tugging his sleeve*) What's up, Charlie?

CHARLIE: A cop!

SAM: Eh? You'll excuse me, ladies an' gents, Honest Sam will have to retire. Careful can't you, Charlie! Do you want to break me blasted neck?

(*He gets down and disappears into the entry. The crowd disperses quickly. A policeman passes*)

HARRY (*left alone with* SALLY): Gosh! I thought he was going to take me up.

SALLY: Not he! The police'll never touch Sam Grundy *or* his customers.

HARRY: Well, I must find Helen and tell her. There you are.

(*He gives her some notes*)

SALLY: Nay, Harry, don't be foolish.

HARRY: Go on, get your shorts, and anything else you've a mind to.

SALLY: Thanks, Harry. So you do like Helen Hawkins after all?

HARRY (*shyly*): Oh, leave us alone, Sal . . .

SALLY: It's nowt to be ashamed on. She's a nice girl.

HARRY: Do you think so? I'm glad. I like her, too.

SALLY: Very much?

HARRY: I suppose so. It happened sudden-like last night.

SALLY: It takes some lads that way. You're only young once, so if I was you I'd take that lass of thine away on holiday.

HARRY: You mean it, Sal? That's what I thought, but . . .

SALLY: Go on with you – get yourselves out of Hanky Park while you've chance. Marlowe's'll give you a week.

HARRY (*feeling the money in his cap*): Gosh! It's like a dream. I bet there's a catch in it, some road. Twenty-two pounds.

SALLY: That'll take y' to Blackpool or the Isle o' Man.

HARRY: Isle o' Man? Phew!

SALLY: You'll spend your money on summat or other, lad, so you may as well spend it on summat y'll remember.

HARRY: I wonder where Helen is now. Funny if she's not heard about me winning.

SALLY: She's heard, all right.

HARRY: Then, where is she?

SALLY: I left her crying her eyes out in back entry behind North Street.

HARRY: Crying? What was she crying for?

SALLY: Because you've won twenty pounds.

HARRY: Crumbs! That's a daft way of showing you're happy.

SALLY: Nay, lad, she's not happy. She thinks she's lost you.

HARRY: Why, she's barmy! Here, I'd best go quick!

(*He is going*)

SALLY: Hey, lad, just a minute. She's not barmy. You be good to her.

HARRY: Aw, that's all right. I'll do me best. Tara!

(*He goes.* SALLY *watches him, and then turns to go the other way.* SAM GRUNDY *emerges from the passage where he has been lurking*)

SAM: How do, Sally. Well, that were a grand bit of luck for your Harry, eh? You can't say as old Sam didn't pay up handsome.

SALLY: I reckon he can afford it. There's plenty more in the bank.

SAM: Ay, you're right. Did lad give you a share, as I told him?

SALLY: That's no business of yours. (*He surveys her*) Well, what you staring at?

SAM: You're a fine lass, Sal Hardcastle.

SALLY: Aach! Let me pass.

SAM: Nay, hold on, not so fast. (*He holds her arm*) Let's have a look at you.

SALLY (*snatching away savagely*): Leave go!

SAM: Aw, Sal, what's up with ye? What have you got against me?

SALLY: Just that I don't want to even talk to the likes of you. Look better if you'd spend more time with your wife 'stead of pestering girls as wouldn't wipe their feet on you.

SAM: Oh, now, Sal, now. That ain't the way to talk to a friend what wants to help you.

SALLY: Fine sort of help you can give a girl. You've helped too many already.

SAM: Gord, Sal! You've got me all wrong. See here. (*He draws out some pound notes*) Take these. I like you, Sal. Honest I do. I'd ... Aw, I'd like you for a pal, that's all. You must be sick of having nowt to wear, and pinching and scraping week after week ... and think what you could have if you wanted. Anythin', Sal. Anything for the asking.

SALLY: You'd better look out if you won't let me be. Just you tell that to Larry Meath.

SAM: Larry Meath? Turning *me* down for that. *Me* an' all I could give y'! Turning me down for a white-livered Bolshie. Yah! You're daft. Huh!

SALLY: That's enough! Leave him out of it. You ain't fit to have his name on your breath. You great fat swine! All as *you* want out of girl is one thing only. But you don't get it out of me. Do you understand?

SAM: Aw, Sal, don't go getting me all wrong. I've a quick temper, that's all. So it's Larry Meath you're set on, is it?

SALLY: That's my business. You mind yours.

(*She is going*)

SAM: He works at Marlowe's, eh?
SALLY: Ay, he works, and it's more'n you ever did. Why?
SAM: That's my business. You mind yours.
SALLY: Aach!

(*She goes.* SAM *stands puffing his cigar thoughtfully*)

SAM: Hey! Charlie!
CHARLIE (*in the entry behind* SAM): Ay?
SAM: Come here.

(CHARLIE *comes out to* SAM's *side.* SAM *talks to him without actually looking at him*)

CHARLIE: Yes, Mr Grundy?
SAM: You know Larry Meath?
CHARLIE: Ay. Works at Marlowe's. He's a fitter. Ay, of course I know him.
SAM: What's he getting?
CHARLIE: About two ten a week, I fancy.[29]
SAM: I want you to take a message to Ted Munter. Ted Munter, you understand, and nobody else. He's allus talking about influence he's got at Marlowe's. And he hasn't settled up that bill yet, has he?
CHARLIE: No, still owing.
SAM: Well, tell him I'd love to see a bit of that influence working, see? And tell him Larry Meath's no pal o' mine. Have y'got it?
CHARLIE: You mean you want Ted Munter to . . .
SAM: Shut your trap! Just remind Ted about his little bill. Tell him if summat happened to Larry Meath on Satur-

day we might consider his bill was settled. Do you see? Go on, hop it! Here's that cop again.

(CHARLIE *goes. The* POLICEMAN *passes back again. He touches his hat to* SAM)

POLICEMAN: Afternoon, Mr Grundy.

SAM: Afternoon. Nice weather.

POLICEMAN: Ay, not so bad.

SAM: Here. Want a tip?

POLICEMAN: A tip? No, thank you, Mr Grundy. I've heard it. *I've* heard it. 'Dusty Carpet', eh? Wants a lot of beating? Ah, you can't take *me* in that road!

(*The* POLICEMAN *goes chuckling.* SAM GRUNDY *remains puffing his cigar*)

CURTAIN

ACT II

SCENE 2

On the moors. A high cleft between the rocks, commanding a view over many miles of moorland country, stretching towards the sunset. SALLY'*s voice is heard, and then* LARRY'*s, as they climb up to the cleft.*

SALLY (*laughing happily*): Oo, Larry, I can't? It's too high!

LARRY: Go on . . . only a few yards, and we're there.

SALLY: Larry, I'm slipping!

LARRY: No, you're not. Up with you! There you are. All right!

SALLY: Yes, I'm up now. (SALLY *appears, in hiking shorts and shirt*) This is the place, Larry. Oo, be careful, you'll slip!

(LARRY *appears*)

LARRY: I'm all right. Don't you worry about me. Well, are you happy now we've got here?

SALLY: Fine! Aren't we high up in the world? This is a special place, and only us two know why. Isn't it grand being alone? I've never seen so much loneliness in all me life.

LARRY (*laughing*): You *are* a funny girl.

SALLY: Be careful, Larry! You give me a turn when you stand right on the edge.

LARRY: Come on, then – hold my hand. Isn't that a grand view?

SALLY: Grand! Miles an' miles of it. Gosh! And this air – it's wonderful. I wish I could breathe it every day. Makes me feel like I could fly.

LARRY: Well, don't do that, or else you'll give *me* a turn. Here, take something to hold you down. One apple left.

SALLY: No, that's yours.

LARRY: You have it, Sal.

SALLY: I couldn't. It's yours. You've eaten nothing yourself.

LARRY: We'll go halves. (*He splits the apple*) There you are, take the red side. It matches your cheeks.

SALLY: Phew! I feel like a beetroot. Wasn't it a climb?

LARRY: Um! We shall never manage to get up here when we're old.

(*They sit down and munch their apple*)

SALLY: It's been lovely today, Larry.

LARRY: You've liked it?

SALLY: You know I have. Haven't you?

LARRY: Of course, it's fine.

SALLY: Larry?

LARRY: Yes, sweetheart?

SALLY: Is there owt wrong?

LARRY: Wrong? No. Nothing could be wrong up here.

SALLY: You're not worried?

LARRY: No, why?

SALLY: You've got a kind of troubled look.

LARRY: Have I? It's nothing.

SALLY: Nowt on your mind?

LARRY: Only you.

SALLY: Your cough's not bad again?

LARRY: No, I'm fine, thanks.

SALLY: Well, you haven't said anything about . . .

LARRY: About what?

SALLY: You haven't said you like me shorts.

LARRY: Haven't I? Why, Sally, you're lovelier than ever.

Perhaps that's why I'm sad today. Beauty makes you feel that way, sometimes.

SALLY: Why?

LARRY: Because when you've lived in a place that's ugly all your life beautiful things seem out of reach. We get to thinking beauty is something forbidden, something that's too good for us . . .

SALLY: You don't feel like that about me, surely?

LARRY: Sometimes.

SALLY: Don't talk soft, Larry. (*She ruffles his hair*) Look at yon sunset. Why is it so red?

LARRY: They say it's the sunshine through the smoke. Hanky Park's over there – thirty miles away. It's a queer thing that all that foul smoke should make beauty for us.

SALLY: See yon cloud – big black fellow with a bulge in him. (*She laughs*) Why, it's Sam Grundy!

LARRY (*laughing, too*): So it is! See, there's his bowler hat, and his cigar.

SALLY: Sky's the limit with honest Sam! Coo-eee! How are you, Sam?

LARRY: I shouldn't make too free with him, Sal.

SALLY: Oh, Larry, I feel like nowt on earth! I feel real mad! And I'm so happy! I've never been so happy in me life.

LARRY: Bless you, Sal!

SALLY: Aren't you happy?

LARRY: Yes . . . if this could last for ever.

SALLY: For ever and ever! Larry . . . ?

LARRY: Yes?

SALLY: We'll come up here – often?

LARRY: Of course.

SALLY: If we could build a house, and live here . . .

LARRY: Goose!

SALLY: . . . and keep this place, just for two of us – sacred . . . Gosh! That's funny talk!

LARRY: Some people call it poetry. Wanting what you can't get. It's the same thing.

SALLY: I'm no poet, Larry, but there's summat in all this loneliness, summat I've been wanting . . . (*A pause*) Larry?

LARRY: Well?

SALLY: Do you believe in – God?

LARRY (*laughing*): Me? Why? What a funny question!

SALLY: Do you, though?

LARRY: Why do you ask that?

SALLY: Oh, I dunno. I've never felt that way before. I've never found owt worth believing in Hanky Park. But it's different up here. Here you belong . . . you belong to summat big – summat grand, summat that it's fine to belong to . . .

LARRY: I know, Sal, I know.

SALLY: But sometimes I get frightened. It's like as if summat up there was saying, 'Take care, Sal Hardcastle, as you don't climb too high and fall'.

LARRY: That's nonsense. But think of those poor devils in Hanky Park who never learn how good life can be. They're as good as dead the day they're born. They're satisfied, because they don't know any better. We can thank heaven, Sal, that *we've* learnt to be discontented.

SALLY: Ay, but we've got to go back. We've got to go back.

LARRY: Yes. We're just two prisoners on ticket-of-leave.[30]

SALLY: Why, oh, why . . . ? There's other places in the world . . .

LARRY: We go back where the money is. Money's our master, Sal, and we're its slaves. There's only one spot in the whole wide world where someone will buy our

labour – our special brand of labour – and that spot's
Hanky Park. You're right – there's no God there, with all
their churches.

SALLY: Larry, we've got to get out.

LARRY (*bitterly*): Yes, climb out roughshod over the others,
but Hanky Park will still be there.

SALLY: Never mind Hanky Park! We'll be wed soon. It's you
and me . . .

LARRY: That's it! You and me and to hell with the others.
Oh, what's the use of talking? I love you, Sally, better
that anything else on the earth . . . but it's no use . . . God,
it's no use!

SALLY: Larry, what's the matter?

LARRY: Nothing . . .

SALLY: There is . . . There's summat hurting you! Tell me
what it is . . .

LARRY: It's nothing. See, there's the others, going down to
the train. We'll have to hurry, Sal.

SALLY: That was strange talk. What do you mean, it's no
use?

LARRY: Let's forget all that. I meant today to be happy.

SALLY: Well, aren't we happy? We'll be wed by the end of
the month, and it won't be a bad house when we've
cleaned it up a bit. You don't know what it means, Larry,
a house of me own. I'll scrub it from top to bottom, and
there won't be a bug left in it when I've finished wi' it.
Not a one.

LARRY (*groans*): Oh!

SALLY: You know, Larry, dreaming about things you can't
have don't get you anywhere. Does it now? I can't
promise curtains yet awhile, we'll have to wait for *them*.
But the room'll look fair decent, what with your books
and the walnut table we saw at Price & Jones's. Come on,

lad, buck up! Besides, it ain't where you live, it's who you live with.

LARRY: Oh, Sal, Sal . . . !

(*He buries his face in his hands*)

SALLY: What's up, lad?

LARRY: Oh . . . I should have told you.

SALLY: Larry, what's wrong?

LARRY: We'll have to put it off, Sally, I'm . . .

SALLY: Put it off?

LARRY: I'm . . . they gave me the sack yesterday.

SALLY: *Larry!*

LARRY: It's true. God knows why, because I thought they needed me.

SALLY: The sack . . .

LARRY: They're turning 'em off every day. I never expected – but of course I had to go.

SALLY (*after a pause, with forced optimism*): You'll get another job.

LARRY: Will I? (*He laughs bitterly*): There's too many out already. Oh, Sal, I should have told you before. But I just wanted to have today with you – and be happy . . .

SALLY: Why can't we be married as we said? There's nowt to stop us. You'd get your dole, and I'm working.

LARRY: No, no, Sal! No, I can't do that.[31]

SALLY: (*taking her hands away*): You mean you don't want?

LARRY: How do you think I'm going to manage on fifteen bob a week? Gosh, dragging us down into that hell of poverty . . .

SALLY: But, Larry, there's nowt for me to live for without you. You don't know what I'd do for you . . . Get house and I'll come and live with you. Who wants to get married? Who cares what folk say?

LARRY: Oh, God, no, Sal! Fifteen bob a week! Do you think
I'm going to sponge on you? Drag you down? What the
devil do you take me for?

SALLY (*hysterically*): Don't talk like that! I'm sick of it all! Is
that all you care for me? Aw, you're driving me barmy.
Why don't them Labour councillors as're allus making a
mug out of you[32] find a job for ye? They're all right, they
are – don't care a damn for us. They've landed good jobs
for 'emselves. And I . . . Oh, I hate you!

(*She throws herself down beside a rock. LARRY looks despon-
dently at the sunset, which has faded rapidly. A faint voice
comes up from the valley*)

VOICES: Coo-eee! Coo-eee! Hey, Larry! Sally! Come down!
It's time to go home . . .

LARRY (*waving his hand*) All right – we're coming. (*He looks
at his watch and then at the crumpled SALLY. He drops on his
knee beside her and touches her shoulder*) Don't, Sal, don't
. . . It's time to go, now, if we're going to catch that train.
Sal . . . I love you, Sal, and there's nothing else matters.
We'll pull through – somehow . . .

(SALLY *turns, and impulsively throws her arms round him*)

SALLY: I'm sorry, Larry . . . I'm sorry . . .

LARRY: That's all right, Sal. I should have told you. I'd no
right to bring you up here . . .

SALLY: Nay, lad, I'm glad we've had today. They can't take
that away from us now. They can take our jobs, but they
can't take away our love. Can they?

LARRY: No, Sal, We've still got that . . . Yes, we've still got
that. (SALLY *shivers*) Why, you're shivering! You're cold.

SALLY: It's different up here now the sun's gone down. I

think this place has changed. It's growing dark – and oh, Larry, I'm afraid ... I'm afraid ...

(*He holds her head close to him and buries his face in her hair. Darkness gathers round them. The* VOICE *calls 'Cooeee!'*)

CURTAIN

ACT III

SCENE 1

The kitchen at No. 17 North Street. A year later. MRS
HARDCASTLE *is seated, darning a sock.* SAM GRUNDY *is on the
sofa. He is obviously ill at ease and has observed convention by
removing his bowler hat, which rests across his left forearm, fat
jewelled fingers curled round the brim.*

MRS HARDCASTLE: [33] So that's what you want, is it?

SAM: I tell you, it's for your own good. What more am I
  asking than that Sal should be my housekeeper down in
  Wales? It's a good job and there's nowt wrong with being
  a housekeeper.

MRS HARDCASTLE: That depends on whose house it is,
  doesn't it?

SAM: Now, then, I'm not having that kind of talk! I might be
  asking the girl to sup a dose of poison. Listen, Mrs
  Hardcastle, I'm not a bad sort of fella really and I've got a
  grand house. Right away in the country it is, with hills
  and mountains and the sea. Just what the girl is needing
  to make her better. Yes, and I've got a conservatory—all
  glass and palms and things. Cost me a lot of brass, that
  house did.

MRS HARDCASTLE (*rising and facing him*): You'd better go
  before Sal comes home, and if my husband finds out—

SAM: Well, what if he does? I've done nowt wrong. There's
  no harm in me offering a job.

MRS HARDCASTLE: No harm, Sam Grundy – but he'd *kill* you
  all the same.

SAM: Look here, Mrs Hardcastle, do you think I don't know
  how to treat the lass well? Me, with a family of my own.

Aw, don't you fret yourself. She wouldn't regret it when I'm gone. I'd make a fair settlement. It ain't as though I've got no brass—

MRS HARDCASTLE: You'd better go.

SAM: You know, Mrs Hardcastle, it's hard on a fellow like me. I'm not an old man, and look at my wife – separated – and she's taken the kids with her. I've got a big house doing nothing and nobody to enjoy it. It's lonely for a fellow like me.

MRS HARDCASTLE: Sam Grundy, I've kept my temper with you so far. I'm not easily roused. But, I tell you, I can't keep my hands off you much longer. You're wanting a housekeeper, are you? Well, you don't get our Sal. I know what you're after, let me tell you this—

(MRS DORBELL *and* MRS BULL *appear in the doorway, overhearing the last words*)

MRS DORBELL: Eee, Mrs Hardcastle! So you've got company.

MRS HARDCASTLE: Mr Grundy was just going.

MRS BULL: Oh, no, he wasn't. You was having words. I heard you. I'm sure it's an honour to have Mr Grundy in to see you.

MRS DORBELL: Well, I suppose we're in the way. (MRS DORBELL *sits on the sofa.* MRS BULL *closes the door and also sits*) Go on with what you were saying. You can trust me with a secret.

SAM: There's no secret. I've made a fair offer. I'm only asking her to talk sense to the lass.

MRS HARDCASTLE: Sense! I may be old-fashioned, Sam Grundy, but I've more sense than to let any daughter of mine be a housekeeper of thine.

MRS BULL: So that's how it is, is it?

MRS DORBELL: Yaah, Sarah Hardcastle, the way you talk. If a

girl don't know which side her bread is buttered, then she blooming well ought to find out! Huh! It's well to be some folks what can pick and choose these days, by gum, it is.

SAM: That's right, Mrs Dorbell. Ay, that's right.

MRS BULL: It's nowt to do with me, Mrs Hardcastle. I reckon it's nowt to do with anybody except Sal. But as for what parson says ... Ach! I never take heed of what *they* say. I've seen too much in my time to be took in by all what parsons'd like you to swallow. I've had no education, but I do know as there never was parson breathed what preached sermon about Resurrection on empty belly, and mine's been empty many a time. Let 'em try clemmin'[34] like us do every day of our lives – parsons' jobs'd be ten a penny then.

SAM: That's right, Mrs Bull, that's right.

MRS BULL: Gar! What do you know about clemmin', you fat porcupine?

MRS DORBELL: He's right, is Mr Grundy. It's a fair offer, and your girl's a fool if she won't take it. Huh! I don't know why you want to waste your time, Mr Grundy. With money you've got, you've no call to go down on your bended knees. That you haven't.

SAM: Oh, it ain't that. When I take an interest in someone, I take an interest. Only speak to her. Tell her what she's missing.

MRS DORBELL: That's right.

SAM: Makes me fair sick to think of her wasting her chances here.

MRS DORBELL: I don't know what the girl's thinking of. Indeed I don't. But I know what she'd do if she was my daughter.

MRS BULL: Ay, she'd land thee a fourpenny one, Mrs Dorbell.

MRS DORBELL: Ho. Would she?

MRS BULL: Ah, keep your hair on. She's doing what I'd do meself if I was her age. Romantic, that's what she is.

MRS DORBELL: Hanging on after that Larry Meath. Why, chap's been on the dole for twelve month now. I don't know what's taken the girl.

SAM (*jingling money in his pocket*): First lass I've met as didn't know the value of brass. I'm only asking you to talk sense to her.

MRS HARDCASTLE (*quietly*): I think you'd better go. All of you.

MRS DORBELL: Ho! If you feel that way about it, after all we've put ourselves out to oblige you . . .

MRS BULL: Mrs Dorbell's disappointed like. She was expecting a commission on the deal.

MRS DORBELL: It's a lie . . .

SAM: Now then, now then.

MRS HARDCASTLE: I said I think you'd better go. Sally'll soon be home, and I wouldn't like her to find you here.

MRS DORBELL: Oh, yes, Sarah Hardcastle! So you've been getting notions from your daughter, have you? Well, I'm doing it for your own good. You know your own business best, but them what's not got a bite to eat in the house can't afford to be high and mighty.

SAM: Well, I've no more time to waste. I'll be going. But think on, Mrs Hardcastle, think on what I've said. (*He goes to the door*) And another thing, don't let that lad of yours get mixed up with yon Unemployment Demonstration they're having. There's going to be trouble, I know. Don't say I didn't warn you. And good day to you.

(*He goes*)

MRS DORBELL: There now. It's like sweeping money off

doorstep. Huh! It's well to be some folk as can afford to have notions. Why, the man's fair made of brass!

MRS HARDCASTLE: And what do you think I'm made of, Mrs Dorbell? Do you think I'm made of cast iron as'd let me daughter be housekeeper to the likes of him?

MRS DORBELL: There's many as'd jump at chance.

MRS BULL: Ay, and her own mother couldn't stop her if she wanted to. She's a will of her own, has that lass.

MRS HARDCASTLE: Sally'll be here soon, and you know she won't be all that pleased to see you.

MRS DORBELL: Still riding her high horse, is she? You mark my words, that girl's going to have a fall, that she is.

MRS HARDCASTLE: Well, she won't fall Sam Grundy's way. Not if I can help it.

MRS DORBELL: Huh! If that's how you act with them as is trying to help you, you'd best be left to yourself. I'm going. And when you find out who your friends are, Sarah Hardcastle, you'll know where to find me. Come on, Mrs Bull, to them as can appreciate us.

(*She goes out*)

MRS BULL: Take no notice of the owd scut, Sarah. But don't you be too sure. We all come a cropper some road or another, and if I had me time over again I know as I'd never turn up me nose at a fat belly so long as it had gold watch-chain hanging on it. Just tell that to your Sal. S'long!

(*She follows* MRS DORBELL. MRS HARDCASTLE *sighs, and, taking off her apron, spreads it on the table and begins to make up a bundle of old clothes and some battered brass candlesticks.* HARRY *comes in from the street. He is thinner and paler, and obviously troubled*)

HARRY (*dully*): Hello, Ma! (*He watches her*) What's that you're doing?

MRS HARDCASTLE: I'm trying to make up a bundle for the pawnshop. Though I wonder whether owd Price'll take them. I'm afeard he'll tell me they ain't worth nothing.

(HARRY *sits by the table and stares at the floor*)

HARRY: Ma . . .

MRS HARDCASTLE: Well?

HARRY: I've got bad news.

MRS HARDCASTLE: What is it?

HARRY: They've knocked me off dole.[35]

MRS HARDCASTLE: They've what?

HARRY: They've knocked me off dole, I tell ye.

MRS HARDCASTLE: But they can't! You're out of collar . . .[36] Ah, you mean they've found you a job?

HARRY: Have they hellerslike! It's Public Assistance Committee. They say benefit's got to stop, 'cause Sally's working and father's getting dole as it is. They say there's enough coming into one house.

MRS HARDCASTLE: But there isn't, Harry! Y'know there isn't. What're we going to do? What'll Sally say? We're living on her earnings as it is.

HARRY: I'm not the only one, neither. But – it's Helen I'm thinking of. You see . . . we were going to get married.

MRS HARDCASTLE: Get married, lad? You've taken leave of your senses.

HARRY: It's no use talking that way, Ma.

MRS HARDCASTLE: What do you mean?

HARRY: I mean we've got to.

MRS HARDCASTLE: You and Helen Hawkins?

HARRY: Ay . . . she's seen doctor . . . We've got to.

MRS HARDCASTLE: You've got to . . . ? Oh, Harry, what'll your father say?

HARRY: That's just it. Look here, Ma, it isn't that I don't want to marry her. I do, I like her, better than – well, anything, and we was planning to marry. We was going to make do on me dole money, and what she's getting herself, and now this happens. If only we can get a start. I'll be drawing dole again when we're wed. And I thought perhaps . . . well, I thought you and Dad'd let her come here, and we could share back room with Sally.

MRS HARDCASTLE: Ay, that's it. Share with Sally. Aren't we all sharing with Sally as it is? She and Larry Meath wanted to get wed just as much as you did. But they didn't go and make fools of theirselves, same as you've done.

HARRY: But I thought I'd have got a job.

MRS HARDCASTLE: Ay, that's what a lot are thinking. But I don't believe there's ever going to be work again.

HARRY: Oh, gosh, Ma, it's driving me barmy. I'm fair ashamed of walking the streets. I feel they're watching me. I've been to twenty places this morning and it's same bloody story all the time. No hands wanted, though they don't usually say it so polite. And look at me clothes. It'll take six months' pay to buy new 'uns. Aw, God, just let me get a job.[37] I don't care if it's on'y half-pay, but give me summat . . .

(HARDCASTLE *comes in from the streets*)

MRS HARDCASTLE: Here's your dad. (*She looks from one to other*)

HARDCASTLE: Well, what's up now?

(HARRY *is silent*)

MRS HARDCASTLE: Come on, speak up, lad. You'd best get it over.

HARDCASTLE: What's he been doing?

MRS HARDCASTLE: It's him and Helen Hawkins.

HARDCASTLE: Eh?

MRS HARDCASTLE: And he's been knocked off his dole money.

HARDCASTLE: What's this about Helen Hawkins?

HARRY: You see Dad, I'll have to marry her, and I thought . . .

HARDCASTLE: You what!

HARRY: I'll have to marry her.

HARDCASTLE: You blasted little fool!

MRS HARDCASTLE: Now, Henry . . .

HARDCASTLE: You, *you* getting wed! And who the devil do you think's going to keep you, eh?

HARRY: I thought, like, that we could come'n live here and get a bed in back room with Sal . . . Until I get a job, I mean.

HARDCASTLE: You *thought*! Yah, you little fool, don't you think there's enough trouble without you bringing more? I'm having no slut like that living here, do you hear me?

HARRY (*warmly*): Hey! I'm not having you calling her a slut. Just you leave her name out of it.

HARDCASTLE (*slowly, as he clenches his fists*): Are *you* threatening *me*?

HARRY: Ay, I am, if you call her names. I'm asking you for nowt. I'm not the only one out of work in this house, remember. Yah, you treat me like as though I was a kid, just acause I've got nowt and I'm out o' work. You didn't talk like this when I was sharing me winnings with you, did you? Chee! Once let me get hold of some money again an' I'll never part with a penny of it. I'm supposed to be a man, I am ... Well, look at me. Ay, and if there was another war you'd call me a man, too. I'd be a bloody hero, then ...

HARDCASTLE: You're bringing no wife here, do you understand? You've made your own bed with y'r nonsense – y'mun lie on it. Go'n stay wi' *her* folk, the low-down lot they are ...

HARRY (*hysterical*): Stop it! Stop it, will you? I don't want to live here. Do you hear? I wouldn't live with *you* if I got chance. You can go to hell! I'm leaving here ...

(*He makes for the door*)

MRS HARDCASTLE: Nay, Harry ... !

HARRY: Yes, I am, I'm leaving! I'm fair sick of it all!

(*He marches out*)

MRS HARDCASTLE: See what you've done! You shouldn't, Henry, you shouldn't ...

HARDCASTLE: Who's master in this house, eh? I'm having no carryings-on in my family. Me father kept respectable, and so did his father before him, and by God I'll keep respectable, too!

MRS HARDCASTLE: But he's only a lad.

HARDCASTLE: Only a lad, is he? Calls himself a man. Well, he can blasted well take the consequences ... Ay, and take 'em somewhere else. Not in my house.

MRS HARDCASTLE: But he can't get a job, an' they've knocked him off dole.

HARDCASTLE: No more can I get a job. No more can any of us. He'll have to get workhouse relief now.[38]

MRS HARDCASTLE: Workhouse relief! No, Henry, no!

HARDCASTLE: It's all the same, any bloomin' road. We're

paupers, living on charity. Dole or workhouse, it's all the same.

MRS HARDCASTLE: All me life I've feared it, and now it's come. Eh, that poor lad ...

(*She weeps*)

HARDCASTLE (*gruffly*): Now, Ma. Now, Ma.

MRS HARDCASTLE: You might have let lad stay on.

HARDCASTLE: I might. There's a lot o' things I might have done. I might have had gumption not to have a family at all. But that lad went out of here with angry words. It's his own doing, and there's an end of it.

MRS HARDCASTLE: I think he loves her, Henry.

HARDCASTLE: Loves? *Love*, did y'say? I'm thinking that's luxury the young 'uns can't afford these days. Eh, Ma, I'm sorry ... I thought to have done better for you. (*As she looks pleadingly at him*) Nay, don't ask me to change me mind. I tell you, Ma, he'll bring no wench in this house.

(*There's a roar of men's voices outside*)

MRS HARDCASTLE: What's that? (*She goes to the window*)

HARDCASTLE: Aw, that's the men gathering for the Demonstration.[39] Fine lot of use that'll be, too.

MRS HARDCASTLE: I'm feared our Harry'll get mixed up in it. Sam Grundy said ...

HARDCASTLE: What's that?

MRS HARDCASTLE: He said there might be trouble.

HARDCASTLE: Where did you see Sam Grundy?

MRS HARDCASTLE: Oh, he just happened to call. He came with Mrs Dorbell. He's wanting a housekeeper.

HARDCASTLE: Wanting a housekeeper, is he? That's a new name for it. See here, Ma, if I catch yon swine hangin' round our Sal again, I'll kill him. I will! I'll kill him if I swing for it!

MRS HARDCASTLE: Don't talk like that, Henry. You know well enough as Sally's promised to Larry Meath. She ain't that kind of a girl, and you ought to be ashamed of yourself thinking that way about your own daughter.

(SALLY *comes in from the street*)

SALLY: They've started Demonstration meeting, Dad, an' Larry's been asking for you.

HARDCASTLE: Then he'll have to wait. I've troubles enough wi'out demonstrating.

SALLY: And I met our Harry on the corner. He told me what's happened.

HARDCASTLE: Oh, he told you, did he?

SALLY: Ay, and I think you might have asked me before you treated him as you did.

HARDCASTLE: What do you mean?

SALLY: Only that it's *my* money as runs this house, and I might have had a word in the lad's favour.

HARDCASTLE: You keep out of this, Sal!

SALLY: I asked Harry to come back, Ma.

HARDCASTLE: You what?

SALLY: I tell you, I asked him to come back.

HARDCASTLE: You interfering little hussy ...

SALLY: All right, keep your hair on. He wouldn't, and he said he'd never be seen dead in here, so I suppose that's that.

HARDCASTLE: Look, here, Sal, I'm boss of this show, and I won't have you interferin' with my business. Do you think I'm havin' a low-down wench living here, and all the neighbours talking ...?

SALLY: If you want to stop the neighbours talking, you'd

have done better to let her come. An' Helen Hawkins isn't a low-down wench, neither. (*There is a knock at the door.* SALLY *opens it*) Here's Larry, Father.

LARRY (*outside*): Can I see Mr Hardcastle for a moment?

(*The sound of an oration and cheering comes from the street*)

SALLY: Come inside, Larry.

(LARRY *is pale and has a distressing cough*)

LARRY: I'd like a word with you, Mr Hardcastle, if you don't mind.

HARDCASTLE: What's trouble now?

LARRY: I want your help. Things aren't going as they ought. Listen to 'em. That organiser fellow's a fool, and I won't answer for what happens if he gets 'em roused. There's police all over the place.

HARDCASTLE: Well, what do you want *me* to do?

LARRY: I want you to be one of the deputation. The Mayor's promised to meet us at the Town Hall, and it's time we were there now, instead of wasting time making daft speeches.

(*He coughs*)

SALLY: You've no right to be out with a cough like that.

LARRY: I'm all right, Sal. Just a bit o' cold. Will you come, Mr Hardcastle? We want some of the older men with a bit of sense.

HARDCASTLE: Ay, I'll come, though a lot of good the whole business'll do us.

MRS HARDCASTLE: Nay, Father, I don't like you going.

HARDCASTLE: I can take care of meself, Ma.

(*An excited* YOUNG MAN,[40] *with a strong Irish accent, appears in the doorway*)

YOUNG MAN: Where's Larry Meath? Is he here?

LARRY: Yes, I'm here. What do you want?

YOUNG MAN: Come on, man, hurry up! The crowd wants to hear you speak.

LARRY: There's no time to waste making daft speeches. Get 'em lined up for the procession. Do you know the Mayor's waiting for us?

YOUNG MAN: Ach! And let him wait! Let him wait our pleasure. We've waited long enough.

LARRY: Look here, I'm just about fed up with you and your talk. Do you know there's a crowd of police down there with truncheons?

YOUNG MAN: Afraid, are you?

LARRY: Of course I'm afraid. Do you think we're going to run our heads into a brick wall? What's a thousand half-starved men against a hundred healthy bobbies? I'm not leading 'em into trouble, if you are.

YOUNG MAN: Yah! Kowtowing to the boss class as usual, Larry Meath. It's hand-in-glove with 'em, you are.

HARDCASTLE: Less of thi gab! Which road are you going?

YOUNG MAN: Past Labour Exchange and down Crosstree Lane.

LARRY: Oh, talk sense, can't you? You've been told we can't go that way. They've got mounted police down there.

YOUNG MAN: Police? To hell with the police! Traitors to their class! Enemies of the workers! The iron heel of a bourgeois aristocracy . . .

LARRY: Don't talk so damned daft! Here, come on with me. Get 'em lined up, and we'll start. We'll . . .

(*He leans against the wall, coughing*)

HARDCASTLE: Here, Larry, me lad, you'd best stay behind.

Get missis and Sal to take you home. You're not fit to be
out with that cough.

LARRY: I'm all right ... and I'm seeing this through.

MRS HARDCASTLE: You're not going, Dad?

HARDCASTLE: 'Course I am. (*to the* YOUNG MAN) Now, then,
Mr Trotski, come on with ye!

YOUNG MAN (*as they go*): Hired assassins of capitalism.
That's what they are. Are we going to bow the knee ... ?

(HARDCASTLE *disappears with the* YOUNG MAN, *who is
talking excitedly*)

LARRY: Gosh, that fellow makes me tired!

SALLY: Do what Dad tells you, Larry. You ought to see a
doctor.

LARRY: I'm all right. Bit short of breath. I'll soon be right.

SALLY (*holding his hand*): Why, you're feverish!

MRS HARDCASTLE: Was our Harry down there?

LARRY: Harry? Yes, I think he was.

MRS HARDCASTLE: Ay, he is and all! The young fool – he's
carrying a banner. Here, just let me get at him!

(*She seizes her shawl and runs down the street*)

SALLY: You're hot and feverish, Larry.[41] I tell you you're
bad. Go home now and get to bed.

LARRY: I can't, Sal, I can't. I've got to see this through.

SALLY: For my sake ... ?

LARRY: No. I can't. It's my show, this, and everything was
going well before those fools started their nonsense. I'm
...

(*He staggers, and she has to steady him*)

SALLY: There! I told ye ... You're bad, real bad!

LARRY: It's nothing, nothing at all. (*He tightens up his belt*)

Getting excited on an empty stomach, that's all. Makes
me light-headed. There. I feel better now.

SALLY: Sit down, then, and rest. (*She forces him into a chair*)
Ah, Larry, Larry, why do you want to go fighting other
people's battles? You've got yourself to think of, and me.
Let other people take care of themselves.

LARRY: No, Sal, no . . . You don't understand. That's what's
caused all this. Every man for himself and let others take
care of themselves. That's what's wrong with the whole
blasted world. Listen to 'em, shouting now they've lost
their dole!

SALLY (*stroking his hair*): Don't talk, Larry. It's rest you
need . . .

LARRY (*leaning against her*): Rest . . . yes, Sal, I could rest if
something inside'd let me. There's peace and quiet with
you.

SALLY: We'll soon be old, Larry, and best part of our life
gone. Is all your fighting and bitterness worth anything at
all?

LARRY: Sometimes I think it isn't. But you don't know the
misery of dreams . . . be glad they don't hurt you . . .

SALLY: Me? Me not know dreams? You don't know what I
dream about you and me. For ages, Larry. Ay, and they
hurt, those dreams.

LARRY: I know. It's wanting decent things and knowing
they'll never be yours that hurts. But listen, Sal . . . (*He
grips her arm*) We've got to keep those dreams. They're
ours, Sal – they're you and me. They're the only precious
things we've got. If we go down, Sal – if Hanky Park gets
us as it gets the rest, it'll be something – something we
shared together . . .

SALLY: Larry!

(*She holds tightly to him. A big drum starts beating down the street, and voices sing the 'Red Flag'.* LARRY *starts up*)

LARRY: Listen! They've started!

SALLY: No, Larry, don't go! Don't go! You're not fit to go . . .

LARRY: I'm all right . . .

SALLY: Come back, Larry!

LARRY (*at the door*): God! The fools!

SALLY: What's the matter?

LARRY: Look at 'em! Straight for the Labour Exchange. It's that damned agitator leading 'em . . .

SALLY: No, Larry, no! Stay here!

LARRY: I've got to head 'em off! (*He goes out*) Hey, where do you think you're going . . . ?

(*He disappears, shouting*)

SALLY: Larry! Larry . . .

(*The door is open, and we see several people running quickly after the demonstration.* MRS BULL *and her friends go by*)

MRS BULL (*as she passes*): Come on, Sally, you'll miss all the fun.

(MRS JIKE *and* MRS DORBELL *pass by, arm-in-arm, singing.* SALLY *stands looking along the street. The singing grows fainter.* HELEN *stands beside* SALLY *in the doorway. She is very tearful*)

HELEN: Can I speak to you, Sal?

SALLY: Come inside, Helen.

HELEN: Are they all out?

SALLY: Ay, there's only me. (*She closes the door*) I'm fair worried about Larry. He's gone with procession, and I'm sure the lad's ill. Well, young woman, what is it? So you're crying, too, are you?

HELEN: I know what you're going to say. You're going to call me names and say it's my fault ...

SALLY: Well, I weren't going to congratulate you, Helen, but I'm not going to call ye names. Got a bit mixed in your dates, didn't you?

HELEN: I don't care what people say. I love Harry, and Harry loves me ...

SALLY: That's the spirit, lass. That's the way to talk. What are you crying for, then, if you feel that way?

HELEN: They've turned me out.

SALLY: Well, our Harry's been turned out, too, so there's a pair of you.

HELEN: Harry? You mean we can't live here?

SALLY: No. Dad won't have you. You see, we're so respectable in North Street, though you wouldn't think it sometimes.

HELEN: But what are we going to do?

SALLY: Well, now you're asking. I'm sorry, Helen. Don't cry, lass. You're not the only one as doesn't know where to turn. I'll do what I can for you.

HELEN: Where's Harry?

SALLY: Harry? He's carrying a banner in the demonstration. And he'll be finding a home in prison cell if he's not careful.

HELEN: If only we could find a room somewhere. I don't care where it is. You see, I've got me job at mill and we could live on that if someone'd take us in. But nobody'll take us in, nobody decent, 'cause we're not married, and we've no money for that.

SALLY: I wonder how much longer we women'll take to learn that living and loving's all a damn swindle? Love's all right on t'Pictures, but love on the dole ain't quite same thing.

HELEN: I won't give up Harry.

SALLY: I'm not asking you to. I reckon that's all part of swindle. We *can't* give 'em up, else wouldn't we have a bit of sense and do without love same as we do without fine clothes and motor cars and champagne? Would we bring children into Hanky Park if we weren't blasted lunatics?

HELEN: Oh, if I'd only known this was going to happen ...

SALLY: Aw, go on, Helen. Look at the silver lining. When you're married they'll be bound to give you money at workhouse. And Harry'll stand a better chance of getting a job when he's wed. They're giving married 'uns a chance before the others wherever you go. Single blokes don't get a smell in.

HELEN: Yes, but ... we can't get married. We've no money for that.

SALLY: Let's see, what does it cost? Is it seven and six? (*She goes to her coat behind the door and takes out her purse*) Or is that a dog licence? Marriage licences last for ever, though, so it's cheaper than keeping dogs. I know some marriages as wouldn't last long if you had to take out a new licence every year.

(*She holds out a ten-shilling note*)

HELEN: Oh, Sally!

SALLY: Here, take it afore I change me mind.

HELEN: Oh, thanks, Sally, thanks!

SALLY: That's all right. If you feel as grateful in ten years' time, you can pay me back. You know where Registrar's office is – in Mill Street? An' take Harry with you.

HELEN: What shall I say?

SALLY: Say you want to get married, of course. They can't eat you.

HELEN: It's not what I'd planned like. I allus thought it'd be in church.

SALLY: Aw, plans are like that. If we'd any sense, we wouldn't make 'em.

(*She opens the door. There is a distant roar of voices*)

HELEN: Well, goodbye, Sally. And . . . you're awfully nice.

(HELEN *kisses* SALLY *impulsively*)

SALLY: That's all right, Helen. And don't fret yourself. Things'll be all right (*She looks down the street*) I wish I knew what was going on down there.

HELEN: I'm going to see where Harry is.

(MRS BULL *is heard shouting*)

MRS BULL: Yah! You big bully! Call yourself a copper? You're a blurry Mussolini, that's what y'are! (MRS BULL *appears, shouting along the street*) And I hope me husband catches you. He could eat two of your size afore his breakfast any day!

SALLY: What's the matter, Mrs Bull?

MRS BULL: Look at him, the big bluebottle! Look at size of his feet! I'd stop indoors with feet like that! (MRS BULL *dodges inside to avoid an angry policeman*) Eh, Sal, it's a bad business! I said no good'd come of it.

SALLY: What's happened?

MRS BULL: You'd best take your rent-book an' follow that lad of thine. You'll want to bail him out with it.

HELEN: Is Harry in it?

MRS BULL: Stay where y'are. Coppers won't let you get past.

SALLY: Has Larry been taken up?

MRS BULL: Ee, I couldn't see who was taken. But there were hundreds o' policemen waiting down by the Labour Exchange.

SALLY: You mean they're fighting?

MRS BULL: Fighting? It's a bloody war!

(MRS HARDCASTLE *appears*)

MRS HARDCASTLE: Oh, my God! I knew summat'd happen. And our Harry and your dad's there in the middle of it.

MRS BULL: Eh, I wish I were a man! I'd show 'em!

MRS HARDCASTLE: And there's no saying what'll happen with your father in his present state. He gets that fierce when his temper's roused . . .

SALLY: I'm going to see for meself . . .

(*She makes for the door*)

MRS HARDCASTLE: Nay, Sal, come back! It's not safe! They're charging into the crowd . . .

SALLY: I must find Larry . . .

(*Police whistles blow. There is a rush of people along the street*)

MRS HARDCASTLE: Come back, Sally!

(MRS JIKE *appears in the doorway carrying a policeman's helmet*)

MRS JIKE: Hey, gels, look what I've got! Shut the door, quick! Eh, what a time I've had! We rolled him in the mud, and I danced on his stummick! It's as good as being in Whitechapel again!

MRS HARDCASTLE: Oh, Mrs Jike! What *have* you been doing?

MRS JIKE (*putting on the helmet and executing a grotesque dance*): 'If you want to know the time, ask a policeman!'

MRS HARDCASTLE: Did you see our Harry?

MRS JIKE: Your Harry? Can't say that I did. I saw the cops taking some blokes off to the cells, and there was some lying on the ground. But the bloke what owned this helmet won't forget Hanky Park in a hurry!

(*Another police whistle blows, and* HARRY *appears breathless, slamming the door behind him. He carries* LARRY'*s cap in his hand. His head is bleeding. There is a clatter of horses in the street*)

MRS HARDCASTLE: Harry! Are you all right?

HARRY: Yes, Ma, *I'm* all right. Listen, mounted police! They were chasing me. Gosh! They charged out with their truncheons ...

MRS HARDCASTLE: Where's your father?

HARRY: I saw him get away. But he laid out two of 'em first. They'd got all their men behind Labour Exchange, and they told us to go round the other road. But yon leader chap refused, and before you could think they were out on us ...

SALLY: What're you doing with that cap? Where did you get it?

HARRY: I picked it up ... it's ...

SALLY: Let me see it. It's Larry's ...

(*There is a knock at the door.* MRS HARDCASTLE *opens it.* MRS DORBELL *stands outside with a* POLICEMAN *behind her.* MRS JIKE *pops the helmet in the oven*)

MRS DORBELL: Is Sally Hardcastle there?

SALLY: Yes, what is it?

MRS DORBELL: You're wanted.

(SALLY *goes to the door*)

SALLY: Who is it?

POLICEMAN: Are you Sally Hardcastle?

SALLY: Yes.

POLICEMAN: You're wanted down the street. There's someone asking for you.

(SALLY *goes with the* POLICEMAN. MRS DORBELL *comes inside*)

MRS DORBELL: Well, did you ever see owt like this?

MRS BULL: What's to do, Mrs Dorbell?

MRS DORBELL: Larry Meath's copped it.

HELEN: Oh!

MRS HARDCASTLE: Have they taken him to the police station?

MRS DORBELL: Hospital, more like. Copper said it were serious. I saw him go down like a ninepin.

HARRY: Ay, I saw it, too, only I didn't want to tell Sally just now. Copper collared hold of Larry, and laid him out.[42] I saw 'im. And Larry was doing nowt, neither, except trying to turn men back.

MRS BULL: Huh! This'll mean six months for Larry Meath.

MRS JIKE: He'll have sent for Sally to bail him out.

MRS BULL: I'll go down for seven days afore my man gets another penny out of me. Let him go to chokey. I've spent money enough on him.

MRS DORBELL: Thank God as I'm a widder and all me fambly's growd up and out of me sight. Dammum! I wouldn't have the worrit of 'em again, not for a king's ransom.

MRS HARDCASTLE: You're sure your dad's all right, Harry?

HARRY: I tell you I saw him get away. But they got Larry, all right. I couldn't do owt to help him, though I tried. They wouldn't let me get near. But I got his cap.

MRS BULL: Fat lot of good that was!

MRS HARDCASTLE: Well, our Sally's got no money to bail him out.

(HARRY *has been peeping through the door*)

MRS HARDCASTLE: Can you see your father, Harry?

HARRY: No, but there's a crowd on the street-corner. Ay, father's there – and Sally, too.

(*The women crowd to the door.* MRS HARDCASTLE *remains inside*)

MRS DORBELL: Let's have a look.

MRS BULL: Look, there, they've got ambulance!

HARRY: Here's Dad, with Sally. They're coming now. Summat's happened, Ma. There's an ambulance.

MRS HARDCASTLE: What is it? What is it?

(*A* POLICEMAN *appears outside holding back the inquisitive crowd.* MR HARDCASTLE *appears with* SALLY *leaning on his arm. He brings her inside, and she sits beside the table staring in front of her*)

MRS HARDCASTLE: Oh, Sal! What is it, Sal?

HARDCASTLE: Let her be, Ma.

MRS HARDCASTLE: What's happened?

HARDCASTLE: Larry . . . he's dead.

(SALLY *sees* LARRY's *cap lying on the table. She draws it towards her*)

SALLY: Larry . . .

HARDCASTLE: Don't, Sal, don't!

SALLY: Well, that's put paid to that. There's nowt but dreams now . . .

(*A silence creeps into the room. The crowd on the pavement stare through the open doorway*)

CURTAIN

ACT III

SCENE 2

The same, six months later. Late afternoon.

MRS BULL, MRS DORBELL *and* MRS JIKE *are sitting round the table, on which is a bottle.* MRS HARDCASTLE *sits apart on the sofa.* MRS JIKE *is playing her concertina, and the trio sing 'The More We Are Together' listlessly and untunefully. As they finish,* MRS HARDCASTLE *sobs loudly.*

MRS DORBELL: 'Ello, more tears.

MRS BULL: Never in all me life did I see such a one as thee for skriking. Lordy, what ails thee now?

MRS HARDCASTLE (*wailing*): What'll become of her? Oh, whatever'll become of her?

MRS BULL: Yah, ain't that just the way of the world, eh? Her dowter gets a sekklement made on her and then her ma wonders what's gunna become of her. Yah, you don't deserve nowt, y'don't. Why don't y'ask what's gunna become of all of us what's left in Hanky Park?

MRS DORBELL: Fuss y'make of it! I reckon she might have gone farther an' fared worse.

MRS HARDCASTLE: It's him. He'll murder her if ever he finds out. I know her father ... and it's such a disgrace! Everbody'll be talking ... I'm feared.

MRS DORBELL: Talk's cheap enough. Have another drop, Mrs Jike?

MRS JIKE: Thank you. I don't mind if I do. Have a drop, Mrs Hardcastle, it'll cheer you up.

MRS HARDCASTLE: No, I don't want any.

MRS JIKE: Strike me pink! You're a nice one to give a little

party. And me trying to be cheerful for you. Drink up,
gels. While you've got it, enjoy it, say I. If it don't go one
way, it'll go another.

MRS BULL: I dunno. Some folk don't know when they *are*
well off. See here, Mrs Hardcastle, she'll take no hurt.
Sally ain't the kind. She'd have been a sight worse off
hanging about here doing nowt but thinking. If you want
to know, it was *me* as hinted to Sam Grundy that she'd
take no hurt if she went away for a while.

MRS HARDCASTLE: You?

MRS JIKE: Ee, Mrs Bull!

MRS BULL: And why not? Three or four months at that there
place of his in Wales, with all nice weather in front of
her – why, woman, she'll be new-made over again. All as
she wants is summat to make her forget. Everlasting
thinking about that Larry Meath ... It's more than flesh
an' blood can stand. Use your head, woman, use your
head.

MRS HARDCASTLE: There's the other thing. Her an' Mr
Grundy. I don't like it ... It's ... it's ... we've allus been
respectable. And now neighbours are all talking.

MRS BULL: Lerrum talk! While they're talking about you
they're leaving other folks be. Your Sally's had a bellyful
of trouble, ay, a proper bellyful. Her pa comes out o'
work and her brother; then the bloke she's set on marry-
ing dies. She's working at mill, and all her money needed
to keep this house going. Yaa! You've been taking too
much for granted, like a few more I knows. You want to
forget yourself for a bit and try to understand how the
young 'uns must feel about all these here goings-on in the
world today. Every cent they earn being took in keeping
their owd folks and any of the family what comes out of
work. If your Sal had gone on brooding as she was, she'd

have done what poor soul did in the next street yesterday. Guardians told him he'd to give five bob to his people what had come under the Means Test, and him married with a wife and family o' his own. An' what did *he* do? Cut his froat an' jumped through bedroom winder, poor soul. You think of that and be cheerful.

(MRS BULL *takes a drink*)

MRS HARDCASTLE: Hush! She's here now.

(SALLY *comes in from the street. She is better dressed than when we saw her before. She enters with studied unconcern and greets the company airily. Her manner has hardened*)

SALLY: Hello, Mrs Bull! And how's Mrs Jike and Mrs Dorbell? Having a good time?
MRS DORBELL: Ah, well, perhaps I'd better be going.

(*She rises*)

SALLY: You've no need to go. Me complaint isn't catching, far as I know. I suppose whole street knows all me business by this time. Well, I ain't ashamed.
MRS BULL: You'd be a damn fool if y'was. (*They sit down again*) Ay, lass, when you get owld as me you'll have learnt that there ain't nowt worth worriting your head about save where next meal's coming from. Bi God, you will.
MRS HARDCASTLE: Where've you been, Sally?
SALLY: I've been to order taxi to take me to the station.
MRS HARDCASTLE: Taxi?
MRS DORBELL: Ee, lass! Taxi in North Street!
MRS HARDCASTLE: You mean it's coming here for you, in front of neighbours?
SALLY: Well, why not?

MRS HARDCASTLE: Have you no feeling for me shame?

SALLY: *Your* shame, Ma. I like that. Thought it was *my* shame that all trouble was about.

MRS HARDCASTLE: Oh, Sal, what's changed you so?

MRS JIKE: Makes it real wicked, don't it? A motor car!

SALLY: Can't be worse than it is. (*She sinks into the rocking chair by the fire, one leg over the chair arm*) It seems to me that things allus turn out different to what you expect. I thought I'd have been married by now. Huh!

MRS DORBELL: Married? You ain't missed nowt with missing that.

MRS JIKE: Getting married's like a bloke wiv a bald head. There's no parting.

SALLY: Well, it ain't for me now. I can't have what I wanted so I've took next best thing. Sick and tired I am of slugging and seeing nowt for it. Never had a holiday in me life, I ain't. But I know what money means now. An' he's got it, an' by God I'll make him pay!

MRS DORBELL: Are you sure Sam Grundy's made sekklement fair and proper? There's nowt like having the brass in your own name.

MRS BULL: Tell the owd scut to mind her own business, Sal.

SALLY: I've seen to that. He's stinking with brass, and he's as daft as the rest of his kind. Ach! What fools they look slobberin' around you. (*She rises and opens her handbag*) But there was nowt doing till I got me own way. He can chuck me over soon as he's mind to, now. (*She hands three pound notes to her mother*) Here, Ma, take em! They won't be the last, either.

MRS HARDCASTLE: N-no lass, I daren't! What'd your father say?

SALLY: Oh, don't *you* start! I'll get enough lip from Dad when he comes in, I reckon. (*She looks at a gold wrist-*

watch) Well, me train's at 5.45, and taxi'll be here soon. I'd best get me things.

(*She goes out on the right*)

MRS HARDCASTLE: Oo, I don't know what's come over her. She ain't the same girl.

MRS BULL: You're right. She is another girl, since Larry died. And a good job, too, or she'd have followed him to an early grave.

MRS JIKE: That'd have been a bit of ready for you, dearie ... layin' her out.

MRS DORBELL: If I'd me time to go over again, I'd never get wed. Marriage, eh? Yaa! You get wed for love, and find you've let yourself in for a seven-day-a-week job where you get no pay.

MRS JIKE (*who has been drinking diligently*): Come on, gels! Let's be happy while we can. You're a long time dead.

(*She seizes her concertina and launches them into a hymn. The door opens and* HARDCASTLE *appears. The music stops. He glares at the three women. They rise uncomfortably*)

HARDCASTLE: Get out of here!

MRS DORBELL: 'Ere, 'ere ... ?

HARDCASTLE: You heard me. Get out!

MRS DORBELL: Ho! Certainly. I've no wish to stay where I'm not wanted. Are you coming, Mrs Bull?

MRS BULL: Come on, Mrs Jike. We'll be going.

(*They go to the door*)

HARDCASTLE (*pointing to the bottle on the table*): And take that rubbish with ye!

(MRS JIKE *takes it eagerly. They go.* HARDCASTLE *shuts the door. His wife watches him fearfully. He leans with one hand against the fireplace, breathing heavily, and gazing into the fire)*

MRS HARDCASTLE: You didn't get that job, then?
HARDCASTLE (*muttering*): Job? Christ!

(He drops his head. MRS HARDCASTLE *lights a candle and draws the blind)*

MRS HARDCASTLE: You're tired, Henry. Sit down.
HARDCASTLE: Where's our Sal?
MRS HARDCASTLE: She's upstairs. Why?
HARDCASTLE: I've been hearing strange tales, that's why.
MRS HARDCASTLE: Ah, folk don't know what they're saying.
HARDCASTLE: There's summat queer going on and, by God, I'm going to find out!
MRS HARDCASTLE: Now, Henry, don't get in a temper. Don't, please . . .

*(*SALLY *comes in. She is very neatly dressed for her departure, and carries a small leather suitcase. She sees her father and they stand looking at each other)*

SALLY: Well?
HARDCASTLE: What's these tales I'm hearing about thee an' Sam Grundy?
SALLY: Well, what about it?
HARDCASTLE: Why . . . ! You brazen slut! Have you got the cheek to stand there an' tell me it's true?
SALLY: Yes, I have.
MRS HARDCASTLE: Nay, Sally, lass, don't . . .
SALLY: It's true, an' I don't care who knows it. Ay, an' I'll tell you summat else. It's sick I am of codging owld clothes to make 'em look summat-like. An' sick I am of

working week after week and seeing nowt for it. I'm sick
of never having nowt but what's been in pawnshops and
crawling with vermin ... Oh, I'm sick of the sight of
Hanky Park and everybody in it ...

MRS HARDCASTLE: Sally!

HARDCASTLE: So you'd go whoring an' make respectable folk
like me and y'ma the talk of the neighbourhood, eh?
Damn you! You ain't fit to be me dowter!

SALLY: Yaa, who cares what folk say? There's none I know
as wouldn't swap places with me if they'd chance. You'd
have me wed, would you? Then tell me where's fellow
round here as can afford it. Them as *is* workin' ain't able
to keep themselves, never heed a wife. Look at yourself
... An' look at our Harry! On workhouse relief and ain't
even got a bed as he can call his own. I suppose I'd be
fit to call your daughter if I was like that and a tribe of kids
at me skirts. Well, can you get our Harry a job? No,
but I can. Yes, me. I'm not respectable, but I've got
influence.

HARDCASTLE: God! I'd have sooner seen you lying dead at
me feet!

SALLY: Dead? Dead, did you say? (*She laughs*) Aren't we all
dead, all of us in Hanky Park ...

HARDCASTLE (*pointing at the door*): Get out! Get out afore I
kill ye!

SALLY: Right! I can do that, too. You kicked Harry out
because he got married and you're kicking me out 'cause I
ain't. You'd have me like all the rest of the women,
working 'emselves to death and getting nowt for it. Look
at me ma! Look at her ...! Well, there ain't no man
breathin', now Larry's gone, as'd get me like *that* – for
him!

HARDCASTLE (*rushing at her*): Aach! You brazen bitch! Take

that! (*He strikes her, and she falls across the couch*) Keep your dirty lying tongue off your mother, do you hear?

(SALLY *lies where she has fallen, sobbing*)

MRS HARDCASTLE (*running to* SALLY): Eh, Father, look what you've done to the lass!

HARDCASTLE: Come away from her, do you hear? Come away!

MRS HARDCASTLE: Nay, she didn't mean owt. Don't cry, lass. You neither of you know what you're saying when you get that way.

(HARDCASTLE *sinks heavily into a chair*)

HARDCASTLE: Haven't I worked all me life, body and soul, to keep a home for her? Haven't I kept meself respectable for her, when God knows I've been near driven to drink with things? And now me own daughter tells me she's a whore – ay, and proud of it, too!

MRS HARDCASTLE: Lad, she's only young – she's only young. Where should we have been all these months if it hadn't been for our Sally? It's her money we've lived on since they knocked you off dole, and well you know it.

HARDCASTLE: Ay, an' well I know it! And well I know as I mean to be boss in me own house.

MRS HARDCASTLE: But the money . . . ?

HARDCASTLE: To hell with money! She's made her own bed, she mun lie on it.

MRS HARDCASTLE: It's your own bed you're making, Henry Hardcastle, when you've driven our Sally out. Your bed and mine. I'm thinking it won't be easy to lie on.

HARDCASTLE: Leave me be! Leave me be! I'm sick of hearing you. God, gimme some work . . . ! Aach!

(He groans and his head falls on the table. There is a sudden impatient knock at the street door. SALLY *sits up and dries her eyes.* MRS HARDCASTLE *opens the door)*

MRS HARDCASTLE: What do you want?

SALLY: Who is it, Ma?

MRS HARDCASTLE: It's our Harry. Hush, lad, your father's in, and he'll not be wanting to see you just now.

HARRY *(outside)*: It's Helen, Ma. She's took bad. I want Mrs Bull.

SALLY: Come in, Harry.

MRS HARDCASTLE *(indicating her husband)*: Hush!

SALLY: I don't care. I've summat to say to him.

*(*HARRY *comes in)*

HARRY: It's Helen. She's gunna have baby ... She says she wants Mrs Bull to come round, soon as she can. Do summat, will you ... do summat!

SALLY: So it's come, has it? Another poor devil for Hanky Park. You might have saved yourselves the trouble, lad. *(She opens her purse)* Here, take this – you'll be needing it.

(She gives him some notes)

HARRY: Eh, Sal! Ta! Where did you get it?

SALLY: Never mind. And take this as well. *(She hands him an envelope)* And here's another for Dad. *(She puts another on the table.* HARDCASTLE *turns away)* I've been keeping it as a surprise for you, like. You've to take these to the East City Bus Offices, and give 'em to Mr Moreland. There'll be a job each for you. But remember, say nowt to nobody how you got it. And give letters to nobody else than Mr Moreland.

HARDCASTLE *(interested in spite of himself)*: Bus offices? Huh!

They don't want nobody there. There's a big notice warning you off. No vacancies, it says.

HARRY: Let's see. That's manager, Mr Moreland – him as Sam Grundy knows . . .

MRS HARDCASTLE: Hush with you!

HARRY (*smiling*): All right! Gosh, can you imagine what Helen'll say? Oh, ta, Sal . . . a job . . . I've got a job . . . you don't know what it means . . . (*He is hysterical*) Ah . . . Oh, ta!

(*He rushes out to hide his tears.* SALLY *picks up her bag and prepares to go. She kisses her mother. She stands looking at her father, who does not turn his head*)

SALLY: I'm sorry, Dad . . . about all this. Things are different now, to what you've been used to, and you've got to face things as they are, not as you'd like 'em to be. We all want a fresh start – that's what Larry said. Well, there's no starting fresh in Hanky Park, an' I'm getting out, quickest road. (HARDCASTLE *stares brokenly before him*) Happen that'll be a good job and here . . . this'll get you a few smokes (*She puts some small change on the table*) Goodbye, Ma, and don't worry.

(*A taxi draws up outside.* MRS DORBELL *pushes open the door*)

MRS DORBELL: Hey! Here's taxi come for your Sally.

(*There is an excited talkative crowd in the darkness outside.* SALLY *stands for a moment, hoping that her father will turn his head. The concertina outside strikes up 'Here Comes the Bride'.* SALLY *bites her lip, and then, drawing herself up proudly, marches out to the taxi. Laughter and jeering are heard. The taxi drives away and the noise dies down.* MRS HARDCASTLE *comes over to her husband*)

MRS HARDCASTLE: Don't take on so, Henry. You've got a job, now. That's summat to be thankful for. Don't be hard on the lass. There's no harm in her, she's only young and self-willed ... She's your daughter ... And the spring-time's coming on. They say country's lovely in the springtime ...[43]

HARDCASTLE (*an angry, beaten man*): Oh, God, I've done me best! I've done me best, haven't I?

CURTAIN

NOTES

The Text

The play was first published by Jonathan Cape in 1935 at
about the same time as the first London production (Janu-
ary 1935). The text of this first edition did not include the
changes made to the script for that London production.
Following the transfer of the play to New York, Ronald
Gow produced the Samuel French (New York) edition of
the play which did away with the phonetic spelling of
Lancashire speech used in the novel and the Cape edition,
and also changed a good deal of the vocabulary (1936). The
Samuel French (London) edition was published in 1938
and is essentially the same as the New York edition. The
present version of the text is based closely upon the
Jonathan Cape original. Some of the changes to the text
which came about during rehearsals for the first London
production have been incorporated (and indicated in the
notes which follow); the phonetic spelling has been partially
reduced (at Ronald Gow's request), but the original vocabulary has been maintained.

Notes on the Text

1 In the original (Cape, 1935) publication, Mrs Hardcastle did not enter here, but later in the scene. The
change is incorporated here. A reason, at the time, for
allowing her an earlier entrance was the engagement
for the London production of Cathleen Nesbitt, a well-
known actress. The political debate (Larry and Voices)
was longer in the first edition but was never played in
full, and this is possibly one of the reasons for Sean
O'Casey's criticism of the play: 'There isn't a character
in it worth a curse, and there isn't a thought worth
remembering' (*Letters*, p. 537). When Ronald Gow
explained that the speech was intended to be largely a
'noise off', O'Casey replied, 'let me be unto him even

as one of those noises off he thinks so very little about' (*Letters*, p. 569).

2 *Sal, when are you coming up on the moors again?:* The Labour Club to which Larry belonged organised rambles in Derbyshire for 'a jolly crowd of young folks' (*Love on the Dole* novel).

3 *And you've never been near us since:* Greenwood describes Sally's feeling about the ramble, in the novel, in this way: 'Then, remembering the kind of people comprising yesterday's company, she found that she was not sure of herself. She felt herself to be greatly inferior to them all. It was as though they belonged to a different species. Somehow she identified them as people who could afford pianos and who could play them; people who lived in houses where there were baths. Their conversation, too, was incomprehensible . . . Yes, they were a class apart, to whom the mention of a pawnshop, she supposed, would be incomprehensible . . . she blushed, ashamed' (novel, p. 99). See also George Orwell in *The Road to Wigan Pier* (1937): 'The first thing that must strike any outside observer is that Socialism in its developed form is a theory confined entirely to the middle classes . . . If a real working man . . . had suddenly walked into their midst, they would have been embarrassed, angry and disgusted; some, I should think, would have fled holding their noses' (pp. 52–3).

4 *at mill:* Sally is 'an insignificant weaver at Marlowe's cotton mills' (novel, p. 138).

5 *. . . and every week sees another hundred of 'em out of work:* In his autobiographical piece, *There Was a Time*, Walter Greenwood describes the unemployed thus: '. . . groups of scarecrow spectres at street corners . . . left out in the cold. The three million registered as being on the dole did not include the debarred who were being supported by parents or married children . . . men and women who had dreamed of Jerusalem in England's green and pleasant land, in spectral ranks of the unemployed, the tarnished face of Empire' (p. 248).

In the novel, the large-scale loss of jobs is blamed on the government's policy of restricting exports to Russia.

6 *Hanky Park:* The name comes from Hankinson Street and its surroundings in Salford, Manchester, where Walter Greenwood was born and brought up. His father was the local barber. He describes the area, in the novel, as 'a jungle of tiny houses cramped and huddled together, the cradles of generations of the future. Places where men and women are born, live and die and pay preposterous rents for the privilege of calling the grimy houses "home" ' (p. 15). Clearly, a central theme of the play is the need of the central characters to 'escape' from this environment and what it does to its community.

7 *I don't know what you're after, proper, only to make things better:* Note, in the novel: 'She could only have blind faith in his beliefs. She resented them, yet, at the same time acknowledged them as a medium, by which, in her eyes, he was elevated by other men' (p. 140). Larry is clearly not meant to be seen as a revolutionary or a rabble-rouser, but as a man aspiring towards self-improvement for himself and his class. It is interesting to note that his speech is markedly more 'correct' than most other characters.

8 *Forty-five bob a week:* Two pounds and twenty-five pence, summed up in the novel in this way: 'ten shillings rent, twenty five shillings food, five shillings coal, gas and insurance, five bob left ... You give a week of your life, every week, so that you might have a hovel for shelter, an insufficiency of food and five bob left over to clothe yourself and your missus in shoddy.' And what, he asks himself, of other things: 'Books, music, brief holidays by seas'? The thought of these things made 'his heart ache with their beauty' (p. 149).

9 *... apprentice racket's a good way of getting it:* Sacking youths as soon as their apprenticeship was over so that they did not have to be paid a full, man's wage. 'Why, the supply of boys was inexhaustible; there were mil-

lions of them at school; Marlowe's could keep going forever. What was to become of him and his when their time was served? Where would openings occur if every firm was playing Marlowe's game? If! A horrible suspicion clutched him. Suppose this present was an already established or new order, that once a fellow came out of his time he remained unemployed for ever!' (novel, pp. 94–5).

10 *What's wrong? . . . healthy ones:* These lines were added for the London production (i.e. not in the Cape edition). Ronald Gow had second thoughts about them, but was persuaded to leave them in by the director. They were found to be particularly useful in establishing the character of Sally as a girl with humour, an essential quality. In the later scene on the moors, Mr Gow further suggests that an actress playing Sally should 'keep a certain lightness' (i.e. Act II, scene 2).

11 *Makes you feel grand being boss of all that power:* In an essay on *Love on the Dole* in *The British Working Class Novel in the Twentieth Century*, Roger Webster comments that Harry identifies himself with the machinery at Marlowe's in order to enhance his own status. Later on in the novel, however, this 'illusion' is lost as Harry comes to see machinery as 'remorseless'. In the play Harry's disillusion with his work at Marlowe's is seen more straightforwardly to do with wages, status among his workmates and uncertain prospects. (Note that he works at Marlowe's engineering works, Sally at Marlowe's cotton mill.)

12 *Mrs Nakkles:* a phonetic spelling of the way Mrs Nattles's name is spoken by Harry. Mrs Nattles is the agent for the 'Good Samaritan Clothing Club', which, in the novel, is owned by Alderman Grumpole. This was a hire-purchase (money-lending) kind of arrangement through which money was borrowed for a purchase, then repaid weekly with interest.

13 *And it isn't 'gev', it's 'gave':* Ronald Gow cleverly associates the presence of Larry's collar with the impact Larry has on her when he is physically present –

Larry 'seemed to demand your best behaviour. You became so very conscious of the loose way of your speech . . .' (novel, p. 88).

14 Sam Grundy is a bookmaker – illegal at the time of the play. He lives outside the Hanky Park district, in a middle-class suburb. He is the nearest the play gets to a 'villain', although he is not the 'cause' of the community's misery; he merely exploits it.

15 *Trade's been turning corner:* The 'slump' has been traced back to 1921 – 'All the events of the inter-war years took place against a huge, dingy, boring and inescapable   backcloth – unemployment'   (Ronald Blythe, *The Age of Illusion*). It is, however, worth noting that in the novel, and in the play, the 'blame' for this state of affairs is placed at the door of 'circumstances', rather than on the middle classes who owned and ran an 'outdated' and 'defunct' (Blythe) economy.

16 *Labour men:* members of the Labour Party. Walter Greenwood describes in his autobiography, *There Was a Time*, how a 'labour man', James Moleyns, influenced him in his youth. Moleyns, it has been suggested, was the model for Larry Meath, 'the gentle agitator' (as a reviewer in *The Times Literary Supplement*, June 1935, called him). Greenwood reports Mrs Moleyns saying the following: 'He'll finish up in Parliament though . . . If somebody gave him the extra little push – I wouldn't be at all surprised if he ended up taking Holy Orders . . . Oh, go on with you, Jim . . . "Christian Socialism" – I did read that article you wrote you know' (p. 174). Jim later comments to Greenwood: 'Unity's the answer, aye, and education.'

17 In the novel, Mr Hardcastle is seen to leave the house deliberately and go 'walking abroad' in order to avoid being asked about the suit by Harry. Harry was unaware that his father's absences from home were contrived: '. . . To Harry, his father's stern visage was a perfect mask: had he known he would have been astounded that his father should be afraid of meeting him' (p. 97).

18 *bout:* without.
19 *Man's work:* 'Youths, young men, men, performing men's work but only being paid boys' wages' (novel, p. 94). Apprenticed boys were being used as cheap labour. Eventually, even those were dismissed 'in their hundreds' and replaced by machinery supervised by unskilled (non-indentured) boy labourers.
20 *three bob poundage:* 15p interest.
21 *the check:* a down payment which covered the interest on the loan, and which had to be paid before the weekly instalments began. Stephen Constantine says in his article in *Literature and History* that *Love on the Dole* shows 'a society living on the margins, facing a grim and unrewarding existence ... The weekly payments were a heavy drain on the family income ...'
22 *Then, who are you angry with?:* Note, Constantine: '*Love on the Dole* makes no attempt to suggest that the middle class were responsible for unemployment and that class conflict was an inevitable or necessary consequence.' Also on this page, Ronald Gow notes that Mr Hardcastle's 'By God!' was altered for the censor to 'By Gum!'
23 *Bird's Eye:* snuff.
24 *th'owld Road:* In the novel, Eccles Old Road 'was the place of residence of many millionaires whose source of wealth was cotton ...' (p. 109).
25 *It's what it does for all the women:* Early on in the novel, Mrs Hardcastle is described as 'an old woman of forty' (p. 16), and later Sally reacts to the 'gloomy Mrs Dorbell, tiny Mrs Jike, fat Mrs Bull' with disgust: 'It did not occur to her that they had been as she now was, young, once upon a time. She saw them as she saw them ... ragged old women, creatures divorced from their species, institutions, as part and parcel of the place as the houses themselves' (pp. 142–3).
26 *Act II, scene 1:* In the French Acting Edition of the play (1938) this scene is replaced by a brief scene in which a drunk Mr Doyle is being hauled off home by his wife. She complains that he wastes his money on

drink while his children are 'starving at home'. The Policeman appears and she is protective towards her husband, explaining that his indigestion is 'somethink awful'. Ronald Gow wrote the Mr and Mrs Doyle scene in for the London production to provide two parts for understudies and to give Act II a more explosive opening – 'it covered the commotion while the audience returned from the bar', he remembers. Given that this present edition is a text for study, Mr Gow has agreed to retain the original scene – although he still thinks it too long and 'too music-hall'. One short cut has been made in the present edition: where the Policeman and Charlie look at the newspaper and note that 'the League of Nations is breaking up', but are more interested in the local football team's centre forward who 'ought to be playing marbles at school' rather than football. The Policeman on his beat is an image which Walter Greenwood used to open and close the novel, illustrating, comments Roger Webster, that 'the inexorable pattern goes on . . . '.

27 *Oh, Harry, let's not fall out:* The relationship between Harry and Helen is of an extra importance to her: 'Didn't he know that his friendship had drawn the teeth of that ogre . . . the squalor and discomfort of her home?' (novel, p. 48). Stephen Constantine points out that Greenwood's sharp distinction between respectable and non-respectable residents of Hanky Park is an important device in enlisting the novel audience's sympathy. The Hawkins family lie at one extreme, the Hardcastle family at the other. Other characters 'combined acceptable and regrettable characteristics' (p. 239). The Hawkins family were 'a low life lot', the mother 'too lazy to cook proper meals: she and her husband too fond of going out boozing' and both indulged in 'drunken sexual behaviour' (novel, p. 65). There were many neglected children: 'One of her brothers, a bow-legged rickety child just able to walk, came out of the house clad only in his shirt. He toddled onto the kerb, and sucking his dirty fingers, made

water down the sough then returned to the house' (novel, pp. 67–8). For Helen, 'reality was too hideous to look upon: it could not be shrouded or titivated for long by the reading of cheap novelettes or the spectacle of films of spacious lives. They were only opiates and left a keener edge on hunger, made more loathsome reality's sores' (novel, p. 69). It seems to me that the extremities of the novel's 'low life' as illustrated by the Hawkins family (and by Tom Hare, who is 'obsessed with matters sexual'; and Bill Simmons, whose bad language is noted; by Maggie Elves, who would 'let y' do owt for a tanner'; and by the threatening Ned Narky) are not so heavily underscored in the play. This is partly due to the practicalities of staging, partly an awareness of the censor, but mostly, I think, because the presentation of the Hardcastle family and Larry Meath on the stage does the job of enlisting audience sympathy without the necessity of a contrast or the danger of alarming what would almost certainly be a middle-class audience.

28 *out of me time:* when Harry's apprenticeship is completed.

29 *About two ten a week, I fancy:* two pounds and fifty pence. Roger Webster makes an interesting point about the importance of money in the novel which can also be applied to the play. He talks of 'the tangle of material and human relationships' and goes on to suggest that money is seen as 'the only arbiter' and is recognised as such, eventually, by Harry and Sally.

30 *We're just two prisoners on ticket-of-leave:* Images of prison feature strongly in the novel: 'The walls of the shops, houses and places of amusement were his [i.e. Harry's] prison walls; lacking money to buy his way into them the doors were all closed against him . . . He was a prisoner at large' (novel, p. 171).

31 *No, no, Sal! No, I can't do that:* An interesting point of discussion about the changing view of men's and women's roles in the family should be possible here. Larry's stance on this issue would be very much

approved of at the time of the play's first performance. In the novel, his thoughts are described thus: 'A humiliating picture of himself living under such an arrangement flashed through his mind. It stank; it smacked of Hanky Park at its worst' (p. 191). See also Mr Hardcastle's feelings about Sally's economic importance to the Hardcastle family.

32 *Making a mug out of you:* taking advantage of him, using him. This links with Sally's description of the middle-class members of the Labour Club described earlier, and Orwell's comments in *The Road to Wigan Pier* (see above, note 3).

33 In the original (Cape, 1935) version of the text, Mrs Hardcastle played a much less prominent role in the opening scene of Act III. The questioning of Sam Grundy and his intentions was left to Mrs Dorbell and Mrs Bull. Ronald Gow felt that it was a weakness to have the two neighbours dominating the action 'as though Mrs Hardcastle accepted them'. In view of their role as a sort of Greek chorus, and the clear distinction between them and Mrs Hardcastle in terms of respectability, Mr Gow is clearly right to prefer the stronger role given to Mrs Hardcastle in the later version.

34 *clemmin':* starving. Neither the play nor the novel says very much about the actual levels of nutrition at the time, apart from referring to the general difficulties of keeping 'body and soul together', as Mrs Hardcastle says. At one point in the novel, Harry grows faint from lack of food and feels 'A vicious fear of deterioration' (p. 172). There is, in fact, much contemporary evidence to suggest that the diet of unemployed families was leading to malnutrition and higher infant mortality. (See S. Constantine, *Unemployment in Britain between the Wars*, London, 1980, pp. 25–36.)

35 *knocked me off dole:* Harry's dole payments have been stopped. This would be as a result of the family Means Test, which was begun in 1931 and involved an unemployed man's total family income being scrutinised by

what was called the Public Assistance Committee. The Means Test was enforced with extreme strictness; the officers of the Committe (the 'Guardians' as they are called in the play) would visit every household, ask a whole variety of personal and even embarrassing questions, and examine all the family's possessions. The Means Test caused enormous resentment and was the direct cause of some of the more aggressive demonstrations and marches of the period. George Orwell wrote in *The Road to Wigan Pier* that 'The Test was an encouragement to the tittle-tale and the informer, the writer of anonymous letters and the local blackmailer; to all sorts of unneighbourliness.' He goes on: 'One man I knew, for instance, was seen feeding his neighbour's chickens while the neighbour was away. It was reported to the authorities that he "had a job feeding chickens" and he had great difficulty refuting this' (see pp. 70 and 71 of *The Road to Wigan Pier* for further examples). Harry's dole would have been stopped because the Committee would feel that the 29*s* 3*d* (about £1.46) per week, which was allowed to a married man with three children, should be enough to keep all the family. To be put back on the dole, Harry would have to move out.

36 *out of collar:* out of work.
37 *Aw, God, just let me get a job:* Note how this is echoed by Henry Hardcastle in the last scene: 'God, gimme some work ...!' George Orwell wrote in *The Road to Wigan Pier*: 'Everyone who saw Greenwood's play *Love on the Dole* must remember that dreadful moment when the poor, good, stupid working man beats on the table and cries out, "O God, send me some work!" This was not dramatic exaggeration, it was a touch from life. That cry must have been uttered, in almost those words, in tens of thousands, perhaps hundreds of thousands of English homes, during the past fifteen years.' Orwell's book was published in 1937.
38 *He'll have to get workhouse relief now:* In the novel Harry is eventually introduced to claiming relief by

Mrs Dorbell with whom he and Helen go to live. She initiates him into approaching the 'Mission to the Respectable and Deserving Poor' and to 'workhouse relief'. He receives 'an order for a half-crown's worth of grocery, printed on the back of which was a list of goods, classed as luxuries, which the shopkeeper was instructed not to supply' (p. 233).

39 *The Demonstration:* At the time of writing the novel (1931) there was a demonstration and march against the Means Test. It took place in Salford on 1 October, involved a march on the Town Hall and ended with a clash between demonstrators and police. The most famous of the 1930s marches, from Jarrow to London, took place in 1936.

40 *An excited Young Man:* it is interesting to note that the Young Man has an Irish accent (it is Scottish in the novel). He is thus identified as an outsider – not one of the Salford working-class and, by implication, moderate community. The leaders of this demonstration are quite clearly shown to be reasonable non-militants. The play's offstage violence is described more fully in the novel, and the police are shown quite clearly to turn the peaceful demonstrators into a mob. 'With the foretaste of constabulary intolerance in mind, Larry feared for the outcome of this demonstration' (novel, p. 202).

41 *You're hot and feverish, Larry:* Larry has in fact got pneumonia and in the novel goes into hospital after being struck down by the police. There he dies. In the first production his cough was played down in case the audience might conclude that he had TB, and also so that he was not thought a 'weakling' (Ronald Gow).

42 *Copper collared hold of Larry, and laid him out:* From the novel: 'He saw Larry standing in the midst of the tussle, an expression of shocked bewilderment on his face. He saw a policeman's hand fall on his collar, a truncheon strike thrice, twice on Larry's back and once on his head. He went down on his knees, head drooping forward. A couple of constables took him under the

armpits and pulled him towards the cells, his legs
dragging behind' (p. 204).

43 *And the springtime's coming on. They say country's
lovely in the springtime ...:* These two lines were cut
from the London production. They were, it was argued, unreal, and Ronald Gow eventually gave way.
He felt that they gave 'a special poignancy to Hardcastle's final speech'.

References

1 *Love on the Dole*, the novel, Jonathan Cape, 1933.
2 *Love on the Dole*, the play, Jonathan Cape, 1935.
3 *Love on the Dole*, an acting edition, Samuel French, 1938.
4 *The Road to Wigan Pier*, George Orwell, Penguin, various
editions.
5 *There Was a Time*, Walter Greenwood, Jonathan Cape,
1967.
6 *The British Working Class Novel in the Twentieth Century*, an
essay therein by Roger Webster about the Greenwood novel
(Edward Arnold, 1984).
7 *The Age of Illusion*, Ronald Blythe, Oxford University Press,
1983.
8 *Literature and History* (the periodical), August 1982, Stephen
Constantine's excellent essay entitled '*Love on the Dole* and
its reception in the 1930s'.

The Walter Greenwood papers are in the University of Salford
Library.

A SUGGESTED CLASSROOM APPROACH

Introduction

What follows is a suggested way into a study of the play. I am assuming a classroom study – and, to those who pick up this volume with production in mind, my apologies – but I trust, nevertheless, that some of the questions may prove useful. The approach is something of a framework for the hard-pressed classroom teacher, rather than an exhaustive analysis. The suggestions can be used for written work or for discussion; the teacher can lead, follow or stand aside. It is a start, which the teacher can choose from, build on or simply ignore. Without witnessing the response to the play, or hearing the questions, this outline is obviously rather abstract – it is not part of the dialogue in the classroom and is therefore unable to react to other voices in shaping the follow-up work.

All questions, and suggestions for writing or discussion, turn the reader back into the text (or the performer back to the evidence on the page), so that a wider, more personal, possibly more creative response is left for the teacher to promote or to guide.

The approach here falls into four main sections. The first consists of detailed questions, aimed at establishing particular rather than generalised responses, whilst at the same time encouraging 'evidence-gathering'. The teacher should know that the questions in this first section are rather 'leading', and can be rearranged according to use. Part II invites the student to try a more imaginative follow-up, with suggestions for an exploration of 'offstage' events, and unspoken thoughts and opinions. The third section is a standard 'lit. crit.' list of longer essay titles. The final section gives some other works which the student might like to look at alongside, or after reading, *Love on the Dole*.

However a detailed study proceeds, I do think there is much to be said for using a reading of this play as an experience which might contribute to a wider examination of some of its issues. For example: unemployment, gender, 'working-class' values and environment, family standards, work, political dissent, 'love', 'dreams of escape', relationships between parents and their children – and even the contribution of drama (and novels/poems) to our understanding of social issues and how far such work can change society. These are all themes which occur in literature quite frequently. What I am suggesting (and not only for the purposes of GCSE) is that *Love on the Dole* has a literary context which our students might explore and profit from.

Part I

The Hardcastle family – establishing their values in Act I

1   MRS HARDCASTLE
   (a) Why does Mrs Hardcastle not want Sally to be seen 'carrying washing in the streets'?
   (b) What does the fact that she takes in washing tell you about her and her way of life?
   (c) What is her view of politics?
   (d) Why do you think Mrs Hardcastle's view of politics is established so firmly at such an early point in the play?
   (e) Are Mrs Hardcastle's feelings towards Larry Meath influenced by his politics?
   (f) How does she react to Sally's desire to buy a pair of shorts?
   (g) How does she feel when she learns that Sally has proposed to Larry?
   (h) What does she think of education? Does this surprise you?
   (i) She says to her husband: 'You won't find it very nice with all them clothes hanging up to dry.' What does this tell you about her relationship with her husband?

(i.e. What is her 'role' in the house? What is his 'role'?)

(j) Why does she join her neighbours in a 'circle'? Does she join in completely – with their conversation or with their activities? Is her role in this scene significant?

2   MR HARDCASTLE

(a) Why does Mrs Hardcastle say, before her husband appears: 'Let's hope your dad stays out a bit'?

(b) Why is Harry nervous about approaching his father for money to buy trousers?

(c) Can you find any evidence to suggest what Mr Hardcastle does when he is out of the house?

(d) How is he treated by the family when he arrives home?

(e) What is his attitude to weekly payments?

(f) Why do you think he gives in to Harry?

(g) Describe Henry Hardcastle's anger. What is he angry about? Whom does he blame?

(h) Do the events of this scene in any way threaten his standards?

(i) Try to sum up his dilemma.

3   LARRY, SALLY AND HANKY PARK

(a) Larry says: 'What's the use of talking to people – they're all too busy with their daft Irish sweeps and their coupons and their betting ...' What evidence can you find in Act I to support this view?

(b) Is there anything in the first act to suggest that some of the residents of Hanky Park have an attitude to weekly payments which differs from the Hardcastle view?

(c) Do Mrs Bull's comments as she enters present a sharp contrast to the Hardcastle family values?

(d) Are the references to drink significant?

(e) What attitudes are expressed concerning pawnshops?

(f) Do you see any evidence to suggest, as Larry thinks,

that some of the inhabitants of Hanky Park have 'given in' to their lot?

(g) What does Larry say about politics and the people of Hanky Park?

(h) Is what he says applicable to Mr Hardcastle? Is it applicable to Mrs Bull?

(i) Sally says: 'I'm one for plain speaking'. What evidence is there in the play that this is true?

'. . . the natural hopes and desires'

1 LARRY AND SALLY

(a) 'You're so different from all the other chaps I've known,' Sally says to Larry.
What does she mean? How has he changed her outlook?

(b) In return Larry says 'you've changed me' to Sally. In what way, do you think?

(c) Why is Larry dissatisfied with Hanky Park?

(d) How do you think that these two characters would define 'happiness'? What would their 'ideal' life be like?

(e) Larry says, in Act II, that just getting out of Hanky Park would not be enough for him. What does he mean?

(f) Describe and comment upon Larry's view of the role of the man and the woman in marriage.

(g) What stands in the way of the marriage of Sally and Larry? Are they right to hold back for these reasons?

2 HARRY AND HELEN

(a) How are Harry's views seen to change, during the course of the play, on the following: girls; his appearance; his work?

(b) Do Harry and Helen see their relationship differently? If so, how?

(c) Would Harry's parents approve of his betting on horses?

(d) Harry and Helen talk about 'dreams' just as Larry and Sally do. Is there a difference in their dreams?

(e) Is Harry's win on the horses a good thing or a bad thing?

(f) Do you think that Harry's relationship with Helen 'works' better than Larry's with Sally? Or is it less successful?

'... the shadow of the dole'

(a) What has the sort of life they have to lead done to Mr and Mrs Hardcastle?

(b) Are Harry and Sally aware of their parents as people who once had 'dreams'?

(c) Describe how Mrs Hardcastle's standards come under attack during Sam Grundy's visit in Act III.

(d) What causes Henry Hardcastle to be quite so angry with Harry when he learns of Helen's pregnancy?

(e) How far do you think that the unemployment situation in Hanky Park is the cause of Harry's dilemma?

(f) What goes wrong with the demonstration?

(g) Sally says to Helen that women are 'swindled'. Does the play show this?

(h) Sally in the last scene of the play is different in some respects. Do you agree? Can you say how? What are we led to believe, looking at the play as a whole, is the cause of the change in Sally?

(i) Comment on the last line of the play. Is this an appropriate thought to leave the audience with as they leave the theatre?

Part II

1 Describe Henry Hardcastle's thoughts (and what he does) during one of those frequent occasions when he is 'out'. (Where does he go? What does he think about? Who does he meet? What does he say? How does he feel about his family?)

2   Write a scene in which Mrs Hardcastle delivers washing to the better-off lady for whom she works. (What do they talk about? Do they get on? Do they understand each other? Do they speak honestly to each other?)

3   Tell the story of Harry and Helen's holiday away from Hanky Park. (Where do they go? How do they react to the change in environment? How do they feel when they have to return?)

4   Write a scene in which Larry confronts his workmates about their apathy.

5   Sally's diary: write three entries for Sally's diary for the following occasions:
    (a) after their day on the moors;
    (b) after Larry's death;
    (c) in Wales with Sam Grundy;

6   Write a newspaper feature about conditions in Hanky Park. (Describe the area, the inhabitants and their living conditions, and the employment situation, and include some brief comments given by some of the characters of the play; remember that they will have differing views.)

7   Imagine that Larry left a letter for Sally. What would it say?

8   If Sally were alive today she would be in her seventies. Imagine you are interviewing her about her youth. What would you ask? How would she reply?

Part III

1   What is the 'Hanky Park bug'? Describe how some of the characters are 'bitten' and how they come to terms with the results.

2   Describe how the Hardcastle family struggle to maintain their respectability. How does this struggle help the play to achieve its ends?

3   Contrast the standards and values of the Hardcastle family with those of their neighbours.

4   What part does politics play in *Love on the Dole*?

5   What view of women does *Love on the Dole* give?

6   Walter Greenwood says in the novel that the people of Hanky Park use 'opiates' to escape reality. What does he mean? Describe these 'opiates' as they are shown in the play, and say how they help or hinder some of the characters.

7   Compare the relationships of Harry and Helen, and Larry and Sally, with a view to explaining what happens to 'love' when people are on the 'dole'.

8   One reviewer said that the play showed a system which had 'ruined men's bodies and killed their minds'. What evidence can you find to support this view?

9   Ronald Gow attributes the success of the play, in part, to its 'fundamental British optimism'. What evidence is there of this in the play? Do you agree with his view?

10   Comment upon the play's 'realism' in terms of: (*a*) its language; (*b*) its characters; and (*c*) its story.

Part IV

For the student:

The Road to Wigan Pier by George Orwell (Penguin)
A Roof over Your Head by Bill Naughton (Blackie)
Buddy by Nigel Hinton (Heinemann)
Escapes by Grazyna Monvid (Heinemann, in the collection *Challenges*)
Boys from the Blackstuff by Alan Bleasdale (Methuen)
Close the Coalhouse Door by Alan Plater (Methuen)
Silent Night by Polly Teale/*Daughters of Albion* by Willy Russell (Heinemann, one volume)
Hobson's Choice by Harold Brighouse (Heinemann)
The Ragged Trousered Philanthropists by Robert Tressell (Panther)
Dockie by Martin Ballard (Heinemann)

For the teacher:

The Age of Illusion by Ronald Blythe (Oxford University Press)

Teaching Controversial Issues, by Robert Stradling, Michael Noctor, Bridget Baines (Edward Arnold)

The English Curriculum: Gender, from the English Centre, Sutherland Street, London SW1

See also references following the Notes.